the
control freak's
guide
to managing life's
uncertainty

Michelle Starr

'The Control Freak's Guide to Managing Life's Uncertainty'
Copyright © 2013 Michelle Starr

Published in Sydney, Australia, 2013 by Starr Guides.

Edited by Sally Salvati
Cover design by Viri Valeria. Copyright © 2012 Michelle Starr
Cartoon illustrations by Mark Martel. Copyright © 2012 Michelle Starr
Author photo by Hans Lignell

ISBN: 978-0-9874631-3-5
Printed in Australia by SOS Print + Media

Disclaimer

This book is designed to provide helpful information and inspiration to readers. The content is the sole expression and opinion of the author who does not represent herself as a licensed psychologist or mental health professional. This book is not meant to be used, nor should it be used, to diagnose or treat any psychological condition. It is sold with the understanding that neither the author nor publisher is engaged to render any type of psychological, health, or any other kind of professional advice. References are provided for informational purposes only and do not constitute endorsement of any websites or other sources. Readers should be aware that the websites listed in this book may change. Readers are advised to use the material contained within this book in a safe and logical manner.

National Library of Australia Cataloguing-in-Publication entry:
Starr, Michelle
The control freak's guide to managing life's uncertainty / Michelle Starr;
cover design, Viri Valeria
ISBN 9780987463135 (pbk)
Self-actualization (Psychology)
Self-help techniques
Other contributors: Martel, Mark.
158.1

About the Author

Michelle Starr is a (mostly) reformed Control Freak, talented navel gazer, and photography enthusiast. She lives in Balmoral Beach, Sydney, where she enjoys seaside strolls and accosting other people's dogs for a cuddle. She has a B.A. Psychology and Philosophy (Hons), works as an Organisational Change Manager, and is a Professional Coach. Having an unrelenting curiosity about what makes people tick, she believes that not taking yourself too seriously can work wonders. While sipping herb tea in her favourite café, she is writing her next book and dabbling in entrepreneurial projects.

This book is dedicated to all those Control Freaks who are afraid to let go and surrender to what is and what's possible. May you find the courage you need to set yourself free.

Contents

Acknowledgements

Thanks to all the people in my life who, through various stages, have loved and supported me, often in spite of my control freakiness.

A huge amount of gratitude to those teachers (H.H. Dalai Lama, Eckhart Tolle, Lao Tzu, Richard Bach, and many others), whose words have inspired me to seek out what's possible and to know myself deeply.

A big hunk of appreciation to Edna, who encouraged me to grow, challenged me to dig deeper, and supported me along the way. And to Dawn and Bec – thanks for being there and believing in me.

To Sally Salvati, my editor and fellow CF, who held my hand through the whole editing process and patiently put up with all of my pedantic requests – your help was invaluable. Thanks to Bec, Dawn and Susannah for reading through the manuscript and providing much needed feedback.

And a massive "thank you" to the talented creatives who made the book look so damned good – Nowitza Milivojevic and Viri Valeria for the cover designs; Mark Martel for cartoon illustrations; and Nebojša Dolovaki who brought all the elements together into a beautifully crafted product.

Introduction

Several years ago, while in the process of pondering my life situation, I came to a surprising personal realisation: that behind many of my thoughts and behaviours was this compelling need to control almost everything around me. At the time, I recalled comments made to me over the years – from those I loved, and those that challenged me to love – and saw for the first time what they really were: desperate attempts to bring even a fraction of awareness to my controlling tendencies. The possibility that I might very well be a Control Freak loomed before me, and in a bid to defend myself against this rather distasteful realisation, I conjured up a number of memories to support my preferred theory – that my character was one which oozed confidence, flexibility, patience and a touch of carefree wisdom. I grasped at anything, any tiny shred of evidence to support this alternative, more comforting belief, in order to alleviate the need to take a good hard look at what this was all about. Try as I did, and boy did I try, I couldn't escape the blatant truth – I was a Control Freak!

This Guide is a result of the knowledge I have gained during my journey into this shadow side of me. Having started off from a highly reluctant, deep-in-denial position, I gradually started noticing when and why I behaved in controlling, dominant ways, and began understanding what 'triggered' my reactions to various situations and people. What I discovered surprised me. The fantasy of who I liked to think I was and the reality of what I came to see in myself were almost polar opposites. My (more than) occasional confusion about the way people perceived and responded to me began making a whole lot of sense when I started looking at situations from their point of view. In short, my Control Freak realisation was a huge wake-up call, radically transforming my perception of life and self.

I realised controlling behaviour is like a coat you outgrew years ago but still feel the need to hang on to, even though it doesn't make any sense to hold on to it anymore. Acknowledging your need to control and letting go of it are never easy steps. Not only does it take a stoic determination to have a good hard look at yourself and the perseverance to keep at it when it's not looking so great, it also requires a commitment to deepen your self-knowledge, and needs patience, understanding and a touch of TLC in dealing with issues that pop up. And, trust me, they will. Once we recognise and accept that fears are the core obstacles standing in the way of our inner peace and happiness, we can then set about the task of addressing what's been holding us back all this time.

The Control Freak's Guide is designed to provide you with more than enough knowledge to understand your controlling characteristics. You'll get a feel for how controlling you (or those around you) are; building your understanding of what drives the need for control. We'll take a look at the stages we go through in learning to acknowledge and accept both our controlling tendencies and the inherent uncertainty within life itself. And for good measure, there are lots of tips and techniques thrown in to enhance your understanding and awareness. Small chunks of humour are hiding in amongst the heavier stuff as a reminder to approach this (pretty intense) topic with a good deal of light-heartedness. Throughout the book, the term 'Control Freak' is often abbreviated to CF to avoid repetitive overdrive. I've also introduced a new term into the English vocabulary (well, at least in this book anyway) – 'control freakiness' – which is a funky way of describing the CF character and its variety of dysfunctional controlling behaviours.

Whatever you take from this book, I hope there's a few "Aha" moments that give you a chance to look deeper into what it is that makes you who you are.

Take heart, you're not alone - CFs are everywhere!!!

"I'm a total control freak and love to participate in the design of every single aspect of life."

Drew Barrymore

"I've always wanted to own and control the primary technology in everything we do."

Steve Jobs

PART ONE

"Who in the world am I? Ah, that's the great puzzle."

Lewis Carroll, *Alice in Wonderland*

ONE

SO, WHAT IS A CONTROL FREAK?

There's no better place to kick off our Control Freak exploration than by seeking out a few definitions to get an idea of how the term is interpreted. Public discourse over recent years has come to denote a Control Freak as a bullish, rigid, even dictatorial individual with a driving need to control everyone and everything around them. It makes sense then that being labelled a CF is typically seen as offensive; it's certainly not conducive to feeling self-confident. It's a rare person indeed (possibly somewhat maladjusted) who gets any pleasure from being called a CF.

For some professional CF definitions, let's turn to those in the know....

Dictionary.com defines a Control Freak as "A person having a strong need for control over people or situations".

Wikipedia states that "A control freak is a derogatory term for a person who attempts to dictate how everything around them is done."

"A person with an obsessive need to be in control of what is happening" is how the **Collins English Dictionary** defines a Control Freak.

Whereas **Cambridge Dictionaries Online** sees a Control Freak as "Someone who is determined to make things happen exactly in the way they want and who tries to make other people do what they want."

"Control Freaks are people who care more than you do about something and won't stop at being pushy to get their way" says **Les Parrott**, professor of clinical psychology.

For **Webster-dictionary.org,** a Control Freak is "Someone with a compulsive desire to exert control over situations and people".

Author of *'Control Freaks'*, **Gerald Piaget** states that a Control Freak is "Someone who consistently controls too much or at the wrong times – someone who needs to be in charge, who can't let go."

It's not too difficult to see the common themes amongst these expert definitions.

Straight from the Horse's Mouth

From my first-hand perspective, a CF is someone who is almost compulsively driven to control those people and situations that have either a direct or indirect impact on their life. This drive isn't always something they're conscious of. It's often like background noise, carrying on despite (even dependent on) their lack of awareness or interest, only noticeable when attention is brought to it.

From an early age, Tina felt a need
to impose order on her environment.

TWO

REALITY CHECK – THE CF QUESTIONNAIRE

Since you have purchased or been given this book, you probably suspect that you or someone you know (wink, wink) might be a Control Freak. But your theory is yet to be confirmed. Now comes crunch time – completing the test that could verify the truth once and for all. There may be a sense of excitement, trepidation (an entirely understandable feeling), or plain indifference when faced with this pivotal moment. People approach this from different perspectives with a variety of feelings. But when all is said and done, the average person would prefer NOT to find out they're a CF. Let's see how you go...

Questionnaire Instructions

The following questionnaire is designed to evaluate if you are really a CF and, if so, what kind of CF you might be. It seeks to determine, in a rather less-than-robust, tongue-in-cheek kind of way, to what degree you have the behavioural traits commonly associated with control freakiness. The questions are best completed when you are feeling relaxed, relatively stress-free, and preferably in an environment that's private, so others won't notice any embarrassing adverse reactions. If you come across a question involving a particular situation that just wouldn't apply to you, resist the temptation to dismiss the entire question and answer it how you would if it did apply.

WARNING: Under absolutely no circumstance should you attempt to complete this assessment if you're feeling on edge, suffering from premenstrual tension, about to lose bowel control, or feeling overly anxious. If these pre-test symptoms persist, grant yourself a self-care break for now and start again when you're feeling a little more at ease.

It became clear that Kristy felt slightly uneasy
about the CF questionnaire.

Question	Your Answer
1. Generally speaking, do you believe that your way is usually the best way?	a) Most of the time b) Depends – sometimes yes, sometimes no c) All of the time d) Not really
2. Your partner has a habit that really irritates you. What do you do?	a) Make it clear that either the habit goes or you do b) Persistently encourage/manipulate/cajole your partner away from their habit c) Learn to accept and love them as they are d) Eventually tolerate it, with outbursts of frustration
3. You decide to go out with your partner/friend for dinner. You:	a) Ask where they'd like to go, then go there b) Simply announce where you'll be going c) Say "I don't feel like that" to any suggestion they make until they finally give up and ask your preference d) Suggest a restaurant, then back it up with positive feedback you've heard (or made up) about it
4. When you're in a disagreement with someone, you:	a) Give in and accept the other person's point of view b) Expect to win and don't give up until you do c) State your opinion but compromise early d) Enjoy the debate - compromise only if it's a no-win situation

Question	Your Answer
5. A work transfer requires you to move to another state or region you've never lived in before. You:	a) Try to convince your employer that the transfer should be negotiable, as the best option overall is for you to stay put b) Eagerly anticipate the change and opportunities that lay ahead c) Refuse point blank – threaten to quit your job d) Prepare yourself by learning all you can about living in the new area
6. You make a mistake in an important hand-written form. What do you do?	a) Carefully use corrective liquid to cover the error b) N/A - you just don't make mistakes c) Throw it away and start all over again d) Scribble out the error or write over it
7. You land an interview for a job you've always wanted. How do you prepare for it?	a) A quick read through your résumé before the interview b) No need to prepare – you'll wing it c) Ask the recruitment agent about the role details d) Memorise your resume, research the company, role play interviews, find networking connections
8. You have friends over for dinner and your partner openly states an awkward or embarrassing truth about you. You:	a) Laugh along at your own idiosyncrasies b) Deny it's the truth (making fun of your partner's ridiculousness) and start an argument afterwards c) Remain silent and withdrawn for the rest of the night, not sure how to recover from the comment d) Feel a tad embarrassed and ask on the sly if that's really true of you

Question	Your Answer
9. Arriving home from a two-day work conference, your partner reveals they've rearranged your favourite room. You:	a) Completely freak out, move the furniture back into its old place, and refuse to speak with your partner until you've cooled down
	b) Ask why they did that without asking, but see if you could eventually get used to it
	c) Appreciate the effort and the fresh difference
	d) Decide to break up – your partner would never be so obviously invasive unless they wanted to break up anyway
10. With your kids now in their teens, you become involved in a discussion with a group of friends about the problems of kids and drugs. Afterwards, you:	a) Make a point of discussing drugs with your kids sometime if/when the need arises
	b) Feel comforted by the fact you rarely allow your kids out to attend teen parties or gatherings
	c) Know you've raised this subject with your kids several times and they're okay to discuss it with you
	d) Consider the option of random drug tests for the purpose of early detection and intervention
11. You've decided to go on a well-deserved overseas holiday. Before you leave you:	a) Book the same reliable place you always go – don't want any unplanned surprises when you're trying to relax and enjoy yourself
	b) Book a trip with a trusted travel company that guarantees a bit of adventure
	c) Look forward to all the unexpected surprises you have when travelling to a place you know relatively little about
	d) Browse the Internet and read a travel guide to become familiar on what you might find there

Question	Your Answer
12. Your computer crashes when you're writing an important document. You:	a) Bleat a few obscenities and anxiously attempt to locate the lost file in an obscure location on your hard drive or USB
	b) Feel comforted and pleased that you save your work after each additional line
	c) Curse your stupidity for not saving the file, don't bother finding a fix, and ruminate over it all day
	d) Accept the loss – lesson learned – and input the information again
13. Issues within an intimate relationship force you way out of your comfort zone. You:	a) Squirm at your partner's offer to seek counselling
	b) Blame your partner – tell them they need to stop being so selfish and change their ways
	c) End the relationship – life's too short
	d) See it as a challenge for your self-growth – bring it on
14. You're invited out for drinks after work with your new team members. After a couple of drinks you:	a) Act normally because you've refrained from alcoholic beverages – can't afford to let your guard down in such a potentially volatile situation
	b) Accidentally get a bit tipsy and freeze as you realise you've opened yourself to a risky situation and are now in dangerous territory
	c) Start to unwind, have a few good laughs and enjoy getting to know your new colleagues
	d) Get a bit worried you may have said a few inappropriate things, but keep drinking anyway

Question	Your Answer
15. You receive a bill for payment that doesn't seem to be correct. You:	a) Never check bill details – it gets paid anyway
	b) Check the bill again but pay it anyway – you probably slipped up somewhere
	c) Contact the supplier and tell them they've made an error – refuse to pay until it's corrected
	d) Double check your entries and call the supplier for an explanation
16. Over dinner, your partner/close friend orders a dessert you're sure they won't like, ignoring the chocolate mousse you know they'd absolutely love. You:	a) Rave about the mousse and hope you've influenced them enough to order it
	b) Respect their adventurous taste buds
	c) Do them a favour – cancel their choice and order them the mousse instead
	d) Question their choice, stating they won't be happy, but eventually give in to their wishes
17. When your partner/friend drives the car with you in it as a passenger, you:	a) Doesn't happen – you're always the driver
	b) Sit there relaxed and enjoy being driven around
	c) Occasionally use the (non-existent) passenger seat brake pedal when you feel a bit tense
	d) Feel the need (actualised or not) to remind the driver of traffic issues and how to handle them
18. You're completely overloaded with work and are getting really stressed out. You:	a) Ask for some help in getting through the load
	b) Buckle down and do whatever it takes to get the work done – no one else could deliver the same quality result
	c) Delegate some of the work to one of your team members then regularly check the quality
	d) Tell your boss the work expectations are unrealistic and request an extension

Question	Your Answer
19. Your partner/friend decides to do something that goes completely against your better judgement. You:	a) Let them know their choice is wrong and that pursuing it is ludicrous b) Give in with some anger still festering away c) Walk away – can't tolerate fools who won't listen d) Realise it's their choice (possibly a viable choice) and respect it
20. It's your best friend's birthday and you're struggling to find the perfect gift. You:	a) Find out what others are giving as presents, then get something fairly similar (but better) b) Buy them a surprise you hope they'll love c) Ask your friend for a list of desirables in priority order and buy something you know they want d) Remember things they've mentioned they liked/ wanted and buy one of those
21. A stranger in the supermarket is about to buy a product you dislike or are vehemently opposed to (for whatever reason). You:	a) Look at the product and give a little shake of your head, perhaps murmuring your distaste b) Probably wouldn't even notice them c) Butt right in and tell them how bad the product is, giving specific details and evidence as to why d) Think about saying something, then realise it's not your business and walk on by
22. Your sister/daughter/ mother/ best friend reveals she's fallen in love with someone you think is completely unsuitable for her. You:	a) Share your concerns, but ultimately respect the choice she eventually makes b) Speak your honest opinion, throwing in a few dire consequences as a warning c) Keep your opinions to yourself – it's her life d) Tell her she's an idiot and refuse contact for an undefined amount of time – teach her a lesson!

Question	Your Answer
23. A shop assistant informs you they don't carry the product you're looking for in their shop. But you remember seeing it there only last week. You:	a) Thank them for checking and take another look yourself b) Ask if they could recheck as you remember seeing it there c) Tell them that they do stock the product and perhaps the manager would be more helpful d) Ask where else it could be purchased
24. You often complain your partner/flatmate doesn't do their fair share of housework. When they do chip in and do something, you:	a) Redo it when they're not around – they've really got no sense of how to do it properly b) Remember to thank them for their efforts c) Buy them a little gift – a reward might make them try a little harder next time d) Are thankful, but notice the lower quality of their work compared to yours
25. You're aggravated when an able-bodied driver parks in the last available disabled parking zone. You:	a) Leave a rather nasty note on their windscreen b) Beep your horn/shake your head and move on c) Chase after the driver and demand they move their car – arguing with them, if necessary d) Probably wouldn't notice or stop to check

THREE

WHAT TYPE OF CONTROL FREAK ARE YOU?

Your Results

Now you've completed the questionnaire, it's time to check your results in the Appendix section at the back of the book. When scoring your responses, try to resist the urge to 'fix' your score based on whom you believe yourself to be (compared to who you really are). Unfortunately, my rather parental (and pretty much ineffective) attempt at preventing cheating by placing the answers in a separate section to the questionnaire isn't always going to succeed. So, for those of you who couldn't resist probing the answers section before finishing the questionnaire, or decided to go back and change your answers based on the results, *add 20 points* to your total score – that is, after all, a pretty obvious clue that some kind of controlling is going on.

Once you've finished checking your responses in the answers section, add up all the points for a total score.

How You Scored

First of all, let's get one thing straight here - the outcome will depend as much on *how* you answered the questionnaire as it does on the responses you've chosen. So you don't delude yourself in any way, shape or form, the following two paragraphs clarify what your questionnaire results will reflect relative to how you approached it.

❖ If you answered the questions truthfully, to the best of your ability, and with a reasonable to high level of self-awareness, the score will conclude that you either:

   a. Honestly have few, if any, CF tendencies; or
   b. Have some significant Control Freak tendencies – you're honest and courageous enough to acknowledge who you are, and so have a good chance of making some lasting changes, if you choose to do so.

❖ If you answered the questions creatively (manipulating some answers) or have a low degree of self-awareness (almost completely oblivious to your true character), the score will conclude that you're either:

   a. In complete denial that you're a CF and answered the questions in a way that reinforces your delusion (oh dear!) – the result will incorrectly conclude you have little/no CF tendencies; or
   b. Lying through your teeth in a vain attempt to absolve yourself of any (perceived) negative traits – the result

will incorrectly conclude you have little/no CF tendencies; or

c. Answered the questions as best (but with a degree of ignorance and/or naivety) as possible – the result could go either way, but will in all probability be inaccurate.

What's Your CF Tag?

Score totals are grouped into four CF levels representing your degree of control freakiness as defined by your total response score. By no means is this a hard and fast analysis of what type of control freakiness you might possess – some people tend to be more controlling in particular situations that may/may not have been included in the questionnaire. What it does do is aim to give you a ball park estimate of the level of your controlling behaviour. Using your total score, check out the CF type that applies to you, as follows:

(25 – 40 points) – The 'Barely There CF'

So you've scored low on the CF questionnaire; chances are that:

- You're probably not much of a CF after all.
- Any CF tendencies that do show up relate only to very specific circumstances.
- You're blissfully unaware of your controlling tendencies, totally lacking the self-awareness to accurately answer the

questionnaire. You're probably wondering why on earth some people have hinted you are a CF – you don't see yourself that way at all.

- You're a closet CF – the worst type of CF – you're aware something's more than a bit awry about your character, but you refuse to acknowledge what it is. Face it, you're chin-deep in cover-up and/or denial. Just couldn't stop yourself creatively manipulating the answers and/or scores to get your preferred outcome, could you?

Notes for the Barely There CF

➢ If you sit fairly and squarely outside the CF box, you probably find it more than a bit challenging mixing with CFs. What's most helpful here is learning how to deal with the (almost inevitable) scenario of crossing paths with a CF. While this Guide directs itself towards helping the CF, you're bound to pick up a few insights here too.

➢ Real non-CFs beware! You're the perfect partner/patsy match for a dominant CF who'd enjoy pulling all your strings and controlling everything you do. The 'opposites attract' rule definitely applies here, but in a borderline dangerous kind of way – don't say you weren't fore-warned.

➢ Check in with yourself – are you seriously devoid of controlling tendencies? Really? *Note*: Check-ins don't work if you're trapped in the quagmire of self-delusion or have only a speck of self-awareness.

➤ Have a heart-to-heart with a couple of close friends – those not likely to be under your controlling influence – do they think you're a Control Freak? If the responses include being overly diplomatic, nervous laughter, jumping off the topic, awkward silences, and sweaty palm wipes, alarm bells should be going off inside your head.

(41 – 62 points) – The 'Situational CF'

Not everyone with a tendency to control wants to do so under all conditions and circumstances. If your test score indicates you've got a milder level of control freakiness, you:

- Probably have a tendency to exhibit CF behaviours, but perhaps only in certain situations (e.g. when stressing out, use of the TV remote control, in-law visits, etc.).

- May not necessarily be viewed as a CF by others; they may see you as someone with quirky behaviours that are more inclined to pop up when things get a fraction too uncomfortable.

- Suddenly realised (with a sense of dread) as you made your way through the questionnaire that far too many of your responses were lining you up for a definitive CF outcome. At some point, you probably pre-reviewed the answers section to check if you were leaning towards a not-so-okay result. And then you probably thought it best to soften the impact by scoring yourself a bit more leniently here and there. Hmmm... not quite ready to face the truth, heh?

Notes for the Situational CF

➢ Because your CF side comes out predominantly in situations that may be emotionally triggering for you, start taking notice of what or who pushes your buttons. There's typically some kind of bodily response that accompanies these triggers (e.g. muscle tension, increased heart rate, face blushing, etc.), and noticing these can be hugely helpful in figuring out just what it is that gets your goat.

➢ Take a good hard look at these triggering situations – being careful not to fall into a bout of analysis-paralysis, which could push you into a rut – and observe what feelings and thoughts rise to the surface at these times. You might find something that unlocks an old trauma or puts you in touch with an outdated coping mechanism you developed when going through difficult times as a teen. Who knows, you could find a few gold nuggets that open up new insights into your character. It's definitely worth a look.

➢ For those of you who gave into the compulsive need to 'fix' your answers, now's the best time to start considering what compelled you to do this; what might be driving you to see yourself as different to who you really are. Just sitting with the discomforting realisation of knowing you're a CF is bound to bring a few hidden issues to the surface. If you're thinking "It's all rubbish", that there's nothing hidden away in your psyche, and there's no discomfort whatsoever, then why the need to 'fix' your answers in the first place? Even though some navel-gazing is sure to stir up things you'd rather avoid entirely, it's time for a major reality check.

(63 – 84 points) – The 'Tad Overbearing CF'

Now we're starting to head into some fairly serious CF territory. This score level is called 'tad overbearing' due to it being so easy for people to spot your controlling behaviour – and you probably do too, unless you're wearing blinkers. If your score fell within this range, chances are:

- You're definitely a CF, and probably one that feels a need for control in many situations, but maybe not all.
- You may be a higher scoring CF that's eased the load by purposely answering some questions less than honestly.

Notes for the Tad Overbearing CF

➢ You've probably been called a CF before, as your controlling behaviours would be well-and-truly noticeable. So it probably doesn't come as much of a shock to you that you are a CF. Have you done anything to date in order to address this rather unpleasant characteristic? If you've done nothing, what's been stopping you?

➢ Self-enquiry is the place to start. Get in touch with that part of you that feels the need to control – look at why and when the behaviour surfaces and what the triggers are. Try writing out some of these experiences in a journal, or taking time out to simply reflect on how you respond in various situations. This helps you build awareness around your character – an absolute necessity for any success in self-transformation.

(85+ points) – The 'Dictator/Megalomaniac CF'

This is full-on, no-holds-barred CF territory. A score in this way-above-average range means:

- Whoa! CF Central Station!! You are one very obvious (and perhaps more than a little scary) CF – the personification of control freakiness. A dictatorial monarch that rules over all – in your own mind anyway. You may not even realise you're so controlling, having ignored the countless responses and feedback you've received about your behaviour over the years, still refusing to change your ways. Or you may be fully aware of how you control just about everything, feeling a sense of security and comfort in this controlling character of yours, completely unwilling to even consider the need for any change. Whichever camp you're in, this requires some serious self-enquiry and an overdose of honesty pills.

- You've completed the questionnaire on behalf of your partner/parent/close friend and are now convinced your perception of that person has now been validated.

Important note: take a good look in the mirror and see if any of these irritating CF behaviours may be hiding within and are simply being projected outwards.

Notes for the Dictator/Megalomaniac CF

➢ WARNING! WARNING! You're in serious CF territory! My hope is that alarm bells and sirens are going off inside your head in deafening tones right now. Something's got to wake you up! What's it going to take?!?

➢ Things just aren't right unless they're done your way, are they? How does it feel to always be the one in control? Powerful? Exhausting? How does your control freakiness impact friends, family or colleagues? Step into someone else's shoes and imagine how interacting with you might feel like – if you can, that is.

➢ Think back on how your controlling behaviours have benefitted and disadvantaged you. Try to be honest in your assessments here. And if you're having trouble getting perspective, ask someone else to help you dig up the nitty gritty of the pros and cons.

➢ Take some time to think about or visualise what it would be like if you just let go of the control strings for a while. What thoughts, feelings and fears come up?

➢ Get a good therapist – NOW!!!

The Generalissimo tended to distance himself
from any perceived form of criticism.

FOUR

EVOLUTION OF CONTROL FREAKINESS

When I first started coming to terms with my own control freakiness, one of the things that kept nagging away at me was a hankering to find out what was behind this compulsive need to control. Believing it crucial to get to the source of the issue, I felt I'd never get a grip on modifying these behaviours if I didn't find this out. My analytical mind initially went into overdrive, as did my zest for self-enquiry, until I finally started understanding the primary drivers.

What the Pros Say

While there are many and varied opinions out there on the complexities that underlie controlling behaviours, common points and themes do exist among them. As a sampler, here are a few opinions from recognised experts on the reasons why people have controlling tendencies (feel free to take on some research yourself):

Expert 1 – Les Parrott, author of '*The Control Freak*':

> *"Let's make this clear: At the root of all controlling behaviour is an attempt to tame our anxiety – not to dominate another person."* [1]

This quote is important for good reason. Most depictions of a CF portray them as people hell-bent on controlling everyone around them with an almost keenly malicious intent – think of the Jack Byrnes character in the 'Meet the Parents' movie series. Truth is, this just isn't the case. By understanding CF motives, we instead see a CF as someone grappling with their own demons, trying to cope with their lot in life, not necessarily someone intentionally trying to screw up other people's lives. Saying that, there are definitely some CFs who do end up deriving a sick pleasure from their controlling outcomes. Guess they spoil it for the rest of us.

Expert 2 – Dr David Schnarch, author of *'Intimacy and Desire'*:

> *"People who can't control themselves control the people around them...When you rely on someone for a positive reflected sense of self, you invariably try to control him or her."* [2]

In his insightful book on relationship 'problems' and solutions, Schnarch hits the nail on the head in his discussion about people who control others. When we don't feel able to control ourselves, whether through ignorance (lack of knowledge), lack of discipline, or loss of confidence, we're more likely to exert our energy outwards in order to manage our anxiety.

Expert 3 – Patricia Evans, author of '*Controlling People*':

> People who control *"are trying to meet a particular need that overrides their good intentions. Misdirected, they have sought to meet this need in extraordinarily destructive ways, even while unaware of the need itself."*[3]

While this CF analysis makes me want to yell out "We're not all acting in 'extraordinarily destructive ways!!!'", I definitely agree there's a 'need' that CFs strive to meet through controlling behaviours.

Expert 4 – Susan Jeffers, author of '*Embracing Uncertainty*':

> *"We live in a society that teaches us to grasp for control, total control, of everything... We insist that life be secure, safe, predictable and all good things. As a result, we are uncomfortable, even panicked, about all the uncertainty in our lives. After all, uncertainty implies 'no control'."*[4]

I really like how Jeffers delivers her assessment on the relationship between uncertainty and control in a clean and simple way. Being in control is generally perceived to be a central prerequisite to succeeding in life, at least in Western society. Any hint of being 'out of control' results in one being labelled as some kind of miscreant, almost verging on the 'immoral'. So to stay well and truly within the 'normal' range of human behaviour, we do our best to demonstrate at least a few signs of self-control. When safety and predictability are of paramount importance, and they are for the vast majority of us, there's little room or need for tolerating uncertainty. To do so requires an ability to accept elements within our environment and adapt to them. A tough ask for some – an almost impossible ask for others.

A (Mostly) Reformed CF's Point-Of-View

In my quest to discover why I was a CF, some fairly major insights were revealed. The stand-out observation that made an enormous impact on my self-perception was this: I noticed that when my controlling behaviour reared its ugly head I was searching for certainty and predictability around something I was anxious about, even if I wasn't consciously aware I was feeling anxious. Why the need for certainty and predictability? Being clear about what's around the corner provided me with a sense of safety and stability, making me better able to deal with the situation at hand and significantly reducing my stress levels.

When you've bent over backwards to creatively control a situation so it suits your preferences, the odds are tilted in your favour that you'll be better able to anticipate the eventual outcome. These situations are, of course, a lot easier to deal with, because there's some knowledge of what's on the way and any required preparation can be taken care of before they eventuate. That's why CFs can seem like some of the most confident people in the world – the reason being that they've controlled everything to the nth degree so they know up front what they're dealing with. Who wouldn't be confident if they knew they could pretty much handle just about anything that might come up?

When life's outcomes feel more than a little beyond your control, there's no guessing what might happen. And not knowing can be a really scary prospect – there's no way of knowing if you're going to be able to deal with the outcome. The more I lacked confidence in my ability to handle or adapt to a situation, the higher the degree of insecurity I felt, the more control I craved. Having an unruly mind doesn't help – all anxiety-riddled CFs have one of these – it cultivates lots of ideas of horribly horrible things that could come to pass that would scare the living daylights out of anyone. So it's easy to see that it's this fear of not being able to cope with life's outcomes which ultimately drives CFs to attempt to control all things in their environment in order to keep their sanity intact. Trying to control my world was my attempt at bubble wrapping myself to avoid all the potential dangers life could throw at me – risk aversion to the max.

Piled on top of all this anxiety around dealing with uncertainty, but closely associated with it, is a fear of surrendering to what is and will be. What do I mean by surrender? Something akin to relinquishing the need to control a circumstance, thing or person; like yielding to whatever opportunities may arise within any given situation, instead of thinking you know the way it should be. I can almost feel your involuntary quivers as you read about the concept of surrender. For the record, the term 'surrender' produces a 'does not compute' indicator in the CF's brain – a state of mind that's strictly off limits. To surrender requires trust – trust in other people, trust that the world will support you, and most importantly, trust in yourself. And trust is a truly challenging concept for us CFs to understand and embrace. We all have trust issues to work through to a greater or lesser degree. Trust, or rather our inability to trust, is at the very core of the compulsion to control, whether we choose to acknowledge it or not.

But Why Control?

In short, controlling behaviours manifest for a primary purpose – to assist in minimising anxiety related to feeling insecure and out of control. As CFs we feel massively unsafe whenever uncertain circumstances have the potential to lead to outcomes which are deemed inappropriate, unacceptable, or undesirable (i.e. anything other than what's wanted). To prevent these dire situations from emerging, we do our very best to shape (read: manipulate) events so our preferred outcomes have a greater chance of coming to fruition. It's considered the best way of keeping our anxiety in check. The more important the outcome, the more control we'll exert over the situation, and the more likely it is we'll try to take control of the entire situation ourselves.

CFs control because we believe it helps us cope with life. We don't know of any other viable way to keep the lid on our anxiety. Our efforts typically get projected outwards (controlling others) instead of inwards (maintaining a healthy self-control). At a core level, we truly don't believe we're capable of dealing effectively with unfavourable consequences. We control others because we lack faith in being able to control ourselves.

In the Beginning…

The origins and reasons for the fears, insecurities, and trust issues associated with controlling behaviour differ from one person to the next. As unique as we all are, the events and circumstances that lend themselves to influencing the development of our behaviours and personality are enormously diverse. One event may not register one iota on our influence register, while another may throw us headfirst into taking on behaviours completely foreign to our character. We're constantly susceptible to a variety of influences (people, societal, environmental) as we attempt to navigate our way through the vast array of complex events that occur throughout our lives.

It doesn't take a qualified psychologist to understand that to maintain emotional equilibrium, we're constantly seeking a balance that minimises or eradicates personal pain, stress and discomfort. In our formative years (birth up to around eight years), we're pretty good at adapting to unfamiliar and unusual circumstances. Not always open to it (as anyone watching a kid throwing a tantrum realises), but certainly adaptable in a wide variety of ways when the need arises. As we continue our path through life, an assortment of coping mechanisms assist us through difficult situations, helping us survive and adapt, and they ultimately shape our personality and behaviours in the process. Sometimes, however, we keep holding on to particular behaviours way past their use-by date, reaching a point where they can become enormously problematic. Although not usually consciously aware of them, we think these coping mechanisms and outdated behaviours help us maintain our emotional balance; at least keep us sane. In reality, they're blocking our path to realising self-fulfilment by locking us into fixed ways of being that make us act more like undisciplined toddlers (who know the best ways to manipulate towards a favoured outcome) than the fully mature adults we're meant to be. Any sense of emotional stability built around dysfunctional behaviours just isn't legit – sooner or later, it'll all come crashing down.

Years ago when I dug around in my psyche in search of answers to where my almost insatiable need for control originated, I found it stemmed from my post-birth adoption. As events go, it first seemed weird and more than a little far-fetched that something that came to pass decades ago, just after I popped into the world, could have such an immense impact on my life and personality. But as I delved further, I accepted that indeed it could have such an impact, and probably did. Being separated from what's stable, safe and known at an early age will inevitably cause a child to find ways of coping with the uncertainty surrounding them. Adults out there with a history of childhood trauma may be all too familiar with the associated trust, abandonment, and security issues, but are yet to discover the knock-on effects it has on everyday behaviours. Self-esteem, encompassing both self-confidence and self-respect, can take a huge beating, with repercussions to practically everything within our lives.

As you can well imagine, outside of adoption there are a wide range of events and situations acting as potential precursors to controlling behaviours, such as: any kind of abuse and/or neglect; losing a parent or close family member; having a parent/caretaker with an addictive personality (e.g. alcoholism, drug addiction); dysfunctional family dynamics; an overly controlling parent; divorce or break up of a family unit; and even moving house often as a child can trigger a desire to steady a life that feels unsafe and out of control. This is by no means an exhaustive list, but it's easy to see how it reflects a common theme of instability and uncertainty. The common link throughout each precursor is the child has to deal with loads of uncertainty caused by people around them and the unpredictable situations that eventuate. They then attempt to adapt by introducing control and predictability into the environment themselves, however they can. These precursors aren't isolated to impacts occurring in childhood years. In fact, any significantly stressful event or trauma at any time throughout life can cause feelings of insecurity and lack of safety, which in turn can manifest as controlling thoughts and behaviours.

From Oz, the Untold Story: in chaotic Emerald City,
it was mischievous young Tommy who secretly
got things under control.

What's Running the Show?

Wherever they originate, our beliefs, values and thoughts push us into thinking and behaving the way we do. Sometimes we have no clue as to what's behind our life's outlook and actions, simply because we have never explored the emotional terrain driving it all. Awareness is the crucial component in getting to know our inner CF. Self-knowledge and mastering the mind is no easy task, but it beats hands-down our often preposterous attempts to try to manipulate and control everything and everyone else.

Negative core beliefs, usually hangovers from the coping mechanisms we learned enduring our unique life experiences, are the crux of the matter as far as controlling behaviours are concerned. Fuelling our thoughts and actions, they are the root source of all manner of anxieties and worries. Failing to nip these in the bud early, negative core beliefs can be annoyingly persistent, hanging around (like a bad smell) for years, and sabotaging our lives in the process. Because they're the driving force behind much of what we do, it's a fine idea to tap into what those beliefs might be. Here's a sample set of negative core beliefs – check if one or two ring true for you:

- I'm unlovable – not worthy of love
- I live in an unsafe and dangerous world
- I'm not good enough
- There's something fundamentally wrong with me

- I'm inferior and powerless
- I'm useless/incompetent/worthless
- My future is hopeless
- I don't matter, I'm invisible.

A belief common to many CFs – the world is an unsafe place – fires up fearful thoughts around anything perceived to be a dangerously uncertain outcome. If there's even a fraction of a hint that pain or discomfort, particularly of the emotional variety, is merely a few uncontrolled steps away, we are highly likely to be feeling especially unsafe, and this propels us into acting out our tried and tested coping behaviours. Facing an unsafe world, we're more-or-less on our own. There are few people, if any, allowed to share a deeply trusting bond with someone afraid the world 'out there' is going to hurt them. People permitted that level of intimacy at some point usually face the inevitable understanding that they will be controlled to some extent in the bounds of this partnership or friendship. Whether they choose to accept that or not is a different matter.

By digging around, there's a distinct possibility a few more core beliefs will pop into view. Another prevailing false belief popular with the CF mind-set relates to a lack of confidence that we can adequately cope with unexpected situations or adverse results. The underlying core belief here is typically some version of "I'm not good enough". With this dismissive tune playing in the background, we don't stand a chance at being able to trust ourselves when dealing with unplanned situations. We try to set up our world so that everything, as much as possible, turns out according to our plans and ultimate benefit. And when something doesn't, we struggle to respond appropriately, often reacting way out of proportion to the loss of control. Such fears around uncertainty can quickly escalate to present a level of threat deemed dangerous, to a greater or lesser degree.

> *"If you don't change your beliefs, your life will be like this forever. Is that good news?"*
>
> W. Somerset Maugham

Our Carefully Crafted Persona

The word 'personality' is derived from the Latin word 'persona' meaning mask or character. Our personality is like a mask we wear that projects what we choose to show the world. Most of us project a self-image that we want people to see – something that is flattering, not undermining. The persona is rarely a true or complete reflection of the authentic character we hide away underneath. This disguise, intended to cast us in the best possible light, hides (or attempts to) all our faults and peculiarities from the world at large. They are masks we expect others will relate to us through; ones that show off our 'best of' characteristics; ones we believe will serve our best interests.

The CF's carefully crafted illusion of being more than 'good enough' is set up to convey an image of composure and control; an over-compensation of sorts. 'Fake it till you make it' is the catch cry here. Just think of all the CFs in positions of power or expertise. Senior management in business is packed with people strutting their stuff, giving off a superior air, when in reality many are just as insecure as the next person (perhaps even more so). It's the proverbial 'tip of the iceberg' scenario – we see only the tiniest portion of the sum total of the person. Beneath the polished veneer lies a firestorm of fearful insecurity. Unsure of their ability to handle life's curve balls, CFs usually feel a strong sense of inadequacy, of not being 'good enough', a lack of self-confidence rarely (if at all) revealed to any but the closest loved ones.

So the scene is perfectly set for playing out the CF's modus operandi – attempts at controlling everything possible and being right ALL the time. And the mask remains firmly in place.

President Johansson gave a stirring presentation on how top CEOs can lead the way in helping staff deal with their insecurities.

FIVE

THE CF LIFE STRUGGLE

A t this point, we CFs are starting to sound very much like highly dysfunctional individuals – in the least, confused; at the most, bordering on sociopathic. You've just read how a CF's need for control can relate to: inner anxiety, an overwhelming fear of uncertainty, difficulty in trusting anyone or anything, feelings of insecurity, and a superficial coating of self-confidence – definitely NOT the kind of info you want to write home about. So as a CF reading this book, which sounds suspiciously like it's suggesting you're pretty screwed up, you're probably freaking out right now!

Before you throw the book in the bin in a fit of angst, first consider this. Reading info of this type can be hugely confronting, and having a reaction to it is completely and utterly normal. It's meant to push buttons. When buttons don't get pushed, we stay switched off to external input and tend to remain stagnant in our comfort zone with zero growth and little chance of fulfilling our potential. Any less-than-pleasant reactions are, in fact, healthy signs – you're feeling challenged to look honestly at yourself and grow. And we all know that when we stretch ourselves (whether physically, mentally or emotionally), there's bound to be some associated growing pain. Most people are averse to the 'no pain, no gain' principle – a throw-back perhaps to the age-old human preference for pleasure over pain. Know that as long as you find ways to support yourself through any process of growth, you will successfully build your (physical, mental, emotion) 'muscles'.

Let's now explore what's behind it all in more depth. Buckle up, the ride's about to take a few dips and sharp corners.

The Veil of Ignorance

Having been bogged down in the mire of the CF mind-set, I know all too well that there's a certain arrogance and sense of superiority associated with being a CF that's not necessarily communicated or picked up on by others. Inside there's a repetitive self-dialogue: "I know the best way"; and as CFs we really believe we do. That's only because there's this huge resistance to and little or no trust in the opinions and decisions others have or make, most particularly those that have a direct impact on us. I mean, why bother seriously deliberating over outside input when yours is clearly better in every way? This background mantra creates inhibitions and close-mindedness which can effectively shut down our access to alternative opinions and possibilities. Even when there is scope enough for considering someone else's idea,

CFs may end up taking it as their own, giving it the required seal of approval needed for acceptance.

Driven by a false sense of confidence and an unwavering belief that nothing or no-one else (including God/Universe/Higher Power) is able to produce the desired outcomes, CFs stick rigidly to time-tested control interventions. This holds true even for those die-hard religious CFs who swear an unshakeable faith in a higher power and honestly believe that surrendering to divine providence comes as second nature to them. Actions stemming from this insatiable desire for control unknowingly reveal to the rest of the world the distinct lack of trust or faith CFs have that anything good can or will unfold without a little assistance. The distrust every CF harbours prevents a natural flow through life, instead replacing it with the anxiety-ridden stop/start characteristics of control. One day in the flow, everything is running smoothly. The next day, a total mess of unexpected events throws everything completely off kilter, and has the CF struggling to maintain any sense of control.

Simply put, CFs believe we're the only ones able to effectively orchestrate the mechanics in life to complete satisfaction. No supernatural power, descended master, spiritual guru, or miracle worker can deliver the goods nearly as well as the CF can. The underlying message here is: "I know what's best for me (and often others) in all situations, events and conditions." Here lies the veil of ignorance – the CF's belief that we're capable of knowing and producing outcomes that reflect life's best offerings, when we're often completely and utterly unaware that what's driving these results is a self-identity based on fear and insecurity. Best outcomes? Not likely. How anyone can honestly trust that thoughts hinged on fearfulness are able to wisely dictate appropriate behaviours is beyond me. But I did exactly that, and I was completely convinced. I knew best. So, for CFs who just don't understand that their controlling tendencies stem from a fearful and intrinsically defective perspective, their blissful ignorance lulls them into a false sense of security and control. Yep, the veil of ignorance is all part and parcel of the CF's distorted reality.

Fred rejected spiritual guidance and empirical knowledge
in the unwavering belief that only he knew how
to reach the heights of success.

Uncomfortable Uncertainty

Life can be oh so frustrating for a CF. Living with the belief that life should afford us a sense of certainty immediately sets us up to experience a whole lot of disappointment. Accepting that life is fundamentally uncertain and changeable is perhaps the biggest obstacle for a CF to overcome. It calls into question not only our perception of how life works, but also has us face our relative impotency in life's bigger picture. People with a tendency to control hold on to believing they're pulling the strings, afraid to even consider believing otherwise in case their world view is completely shattered.

The need to be right raises its ugly head when beliefs hold such fundamental importance to our character, in a way defining who we are – our concept of self. We grasp onto these beliefs, hesitant to let them go or question them in case the 'me' we've built up over the years starts unravelling in the process. Closing off to all other opinions and possibilities is a way of shielding ourselves from a truth that doesn't fit a carefully contrived point of view, helping us maintain a stronger self-identity. At the same time, it shuts us off from differing perspectives – outlooks which can open us up to broader opportunities and help turn on our empathy 'walk-in-another-person's-shoes' switch. We end up boxing ourselves in, stifling our creativity and innovation, all so we can keep a solid grip on the 'me' we think we are (as dysfunctional as that 'me' may be).

Expecting that desired outcomes can be guaranteed through controlling everything ultimately sets us up for failure over and again. Sure, we can influence outcomes, particularly when it comes to how we respond and behave within situations – I'm a big supporter of setting a personal vision, goals and even a daily intention – but there will always be circumstances where elements lay outside of our control, especially when they involve other people with independent behaviours, directions and objectives. CFs have a lot riding on the belief that life can be controlled to the nth degree. Our whole way of being in the world is dictated by and dependent on this belief. So when an end result doesn't fit in with our plans, it just doesn't compute. We think the failure to attain the desired outcome was a result of not trying hard enough. So the control notch is ramped up a little higher the next time, which sadly only serves to reinforce a dependency on controlling behaviours.

Even nowadays I struggle at times to accept that life can't be controlled to suit my every whim and desire. To reinforce the point, life often throws me a curve ball, a not-so-subtle reminder that I'm not the designated driver in every situation. Certainly a healthy way to keep your ego in check. It's good practice to remind ourselves that we don't always know what outcomes are the most beneficial for our own growth and happiness. What we may consider to be life's absolute disasters can often turn out to be some of the greatest lessons we can learn; yet other outcomes we've yearned to achieve do nothing to help us grow when we finally accomplish them, and can even serve to enlarge an already inflated ego.

The fact is, life doesn't always work out the way we want it to. Full stop. End of story. We can struggle with that simple reality and rack our brains over how to make something work, but there's one primary flaw to this logic. Simply put, due to the vagaries surrounding life's uncertainties, we can never manage to control all external (or internal for that matter) influences to the extent of being able to 100% guarantee the result we want will come to pass. Not even the most deluded megalomaniac can achieve that rate of success. At some point, we need to jump into acceptance mode and start letting go.

Stuck in the Comfort Zone

Comfort zones are like beds of security and ease where we feel less of a need to stand guard. Staying inside them allows us to relax quite a bit more than we normally would. We feel less anxious and more able to drop our defences. With this in mind, consider how rare it is for a CF to intentionally step outside their comfort zone. It usually occurs only when we're positive we can anticipate and deal with any deviations from the norm that could arise. Like everyone else, as CFs we just want to live our idea of a perfect life. These ideas, however, usually have an extremely high degree of certainty, no/low amount of anxiety, no nasty surprises, and wonderful outcomes every time. No wonder it takes so much effort keeping it all handled!

Nestled inside the comfort zone, there's rarely a cause for anxiety levels to peak. With a vested interest in ensuring things turn out the way we planned, CFs stick rigidly to behavioural routines that help us minimise the risks around an event or activity. It's kind of like wrapping ourselves up in bubble wrap in order to ward off any chance of injury – we shield ourselves so well, we rarely get to fully experience or feel what's happening. If we don't stick to our routines, a fear for our security may be triggered that can be paramount to a fear for our very survival. Unfamiliar or ambiguous situations cause a huge increase in tension within CFs, generating inner conflict we may struggle to manage. Inside, alarm bells start firing off as the dangers of being vulnerable to serious risk and personal threat become real. Here, CFs can't possibly know exactly what will happen or how we're meant to respond. If the tension becomes unmanageable, CFs will escape (e.g. through addictions or avoidance), explode (e.g. anger/rage towards others or attacks on self), have an anxiety attack or a breakdown. That's why it feels so much better to just keep it all contained in the first place.

The Hyper-Vigilant State

Humans have a serious perspective limitation – when we focus on one element of a situation, we tend to miss lots of other cues and happenings going on around us. Using mind filters to sift out whatever we consider frivolous or unimportant in our world, we zero in on what we consider to be the important stuff. This creates our unique perspective of the world. But it can also make life a nightmare for those constantly on the lookout for threats and surprises they'd prefer to avoid altogether. If our filters are set on maximising self-protection and control, our attention is constantly on the lookout for potential dangers and negatives. A unique opportunity or periodic glimpses of subtle beauty could be unfolding right before our very eyes and chances are we'd miss it completely.

Heightened alertness to anything seen as potentially threatening or anxiety-causing is called hyper-vigilance – a common state for CFs. Feeling the need to be constantly on guard for whatever could present as a threat or menace, CFs have a magnified sensitivity to what's going on around them. This hyper-vigilance isn't always openly apparent to CFs; we're usually quite oblivious to our background fears humming away unnoticed, similar to the white noise that permeates our household environment. A CF's hyper-vigilance is never questioned as it generally remains undetected due to a lack of self-awareness. So any controlling behaviours generated in response to tracking down threats also go largely unrecognised and unquestioned. For those CFs who have become aware of this tendency, the habitual need to be on the lookout for danger wherever it may strike is considered a normal behavioural reaction. Super-sensitivity and hyper-vigilance are CF auto-pilot responses, as natural as the air we breathe, and usually something that's been with us for as far back as we can remember.

When living life through a hyper-vigilant mental state, we think we're operating in our own best interests. Truth is we're denying ourselves lots of opportunities to let go of our fears and anxieties and really enjoy life. Aware or not, we look out for what could potentially get in the way of our carefully constructed plans and desired scenarios. Like horses with blinkers on, we can only see straight ahead of us, totally missing out on everything going on in our periphery. In that sense, while we may be on track to having our needs and wants fulfilled, we're also blocking out great chunks of life going on around us. Forget about stopping to smell the roses along the way – this is an incredibly limiting way of being in the world.

Yes, hyper-vigilance can keep us focused and reduce the probability of unfavourable events occurring, but there's a catch here, and a big one at that. While this super-sensitivity alerts us to certain types of cues going on in our environment, it can also make us more than a bit nervous, even a tad jittery. Because this sensitivity is driven by fear and an almost desperate need to know what might come about, we can read all kinds of things into the most innocent of happenings – serendipitous encounters and innocuous dialogue included. There's a tendency to jump on something 'just in case' it could turn foul, severely restricting the events we allow into our life, and almost completely eradicating any chance for surprise or adventure to show up. CFs think we're being careful and diligent in controlling the chance of risky outcomes; everyone else thinks we're being alarmist or just plain paranoid.

While operating in a hyper-vigilant state we can never truly experience a state of calm, and nothing and no-one is above suspicion. This outlook only helps to create a life centred on doom-and-gloom scenarios. It just doesn't have to be this hard.

"Mission Control, I repeat, have entered
extremely hostile territory! Am under direct attack!"

(SIX)

PROS AND CONS OF CONTROL FREAKINESS

L iving a CF's life is not all doom and gloom, nor is it anywhere near blissful contentment. It's more like the proverbial bed of roses – looks lovely to lie in, but those hidden thorns can sure be painful. Let's face it, in many ways it feels good to be in control, getting our way much of the time. But we'd be deceiving ourselves by thinking there are next-to-no side effects of control freakiness.

On The Plus Side

If controlling behaviours repeatedly brought misery and grief to your doorstep, there'd be CFs lining up in droves to find out how to permanently eradicate such a festering mental ailment. But as that's not the case, there has to be some kind of payoff, right?

Here are several benefits of control freakiness:

- CF personalities are typically very successful in the business world, which traditionally caters to and rewards controlling behaviours. Haven't we all had a CF boss or work colleague at some stage?

- While not always consciously recognised, the CF's controlling behaviours help reduce the anxieties they feel. That is, until the next time they arise.

- CFs often have a high degree of clarity around what's required to create desired outcomes. They can plan, organise, plot, and scheme really, really well.

- CFs have a sharp focus on achieving the outcomes they desire – a single-pointed dogged determination. Simply the best weapon in the arsenal of goal achievement.

- Their personal success expectations and achievement bar can be set higher due to their ability to deliver what it is they think they need/want in life. Because of the outcomes produced, high-achieving CFs often live a life envied by those around them.

- CFs are usually the top performers or specialists in their field.

- They know exactly what's going on – CFs have their eye on the ball at all times so nothing catches them by surprise. In this sense, they can be a useful team resource, especially if you want to make sure nothing gets dropped.

CFs know what they want and they focus on getting exactly that. There's usually a stubborn determination to manifest what they perceive to be the best outcomes. This aligns itself well with the principles around the goal-setting and creating-the-life-you-want approaches touted by personal development gurus. Seemingly perfect for this age of restless self-indulgence and higher-than-ever expectations. CFs constantly have their behaviours reinforced, because the benefits outlined above are highly valued in this goal-oriented world.

"...And that in a nutshell is how we shall capture
the 2 p.m. conference room slot."

On the Down Side

But there's a down side too. Behind the veneer of success and self-assurance, CFs are a bundle of insecurity, afraid to let go of their stranglehold on how things should be and live life to the fullest. Even if it's not exactly evident on the surface, they're nervous, anxious, and incredibly fearful if things don't go the way they envisioned. When insecurities are the platform from which you create your life, it's kind of like building a home on quicksand – sooner or later, something's going to give and the whole thing will topple over.

Spending huge amounts of time and energy controlling situations and people, in an attempt to make life as perfect as possible, takes its toll in more ways than one. Here's a summary of the disadvantages of being a CF:

- CFs miss so much of the 'good' stuff while worrying themselves silly making sure the 'bad' stuff doesn't come up to bite them.
- They have difficulty in maintaining intimate relationships, including close friendships.
- Needing to control everything all the time can be emotionally and physically exhausting.
- While constantly keeping the wolves at bay, CFs rarely get to enjoy life and all it has to offer.
- CFs face challenges when connecting into the bigger picture – by focusing predominantly on life's potential negatives, they develop a severely limited in-the-box perspective.

- What CFs want, and are often hell-bent on attaining, doesn't necessarily equate with what they need to become mature, healthy and relatively stress-free adults.

- Unless risks are highly calculated and end impacts deemed minimal, CFs are generally risk averse. This often results in a very controlled and predictable (read: boring) life.

- While CFs do get some respect for what they achieve, they aren't necessarily respected for *how* they've achieved it or for the kind of person they show themselves to be.

- CFs become dependent on their controlling behaviours as a way of keeping anxiety at bay. The message – anxiety can only be stopped when I'm in control. But controlling doesn't do anything to address the core issues behind the anxiety. It's merely a Band-Aid solution; a short-term fix that ends up exacerbating their CF nature.

- People grow tired of having a CF try to control everything they do – many people will eventually choose not to associate with the CF.

- Clued in people around the CF know they're filled with fear and anxiety. It's like a semi-invisible sign on their forehead that reads: "I'm an insecure Control Freak."

Most of the time, CFs just don't see the down side. Despite the fact the disadvantages of being controlling are pretty obvious to all and sundry around them, CFs choose to focus predominantly on the more positive effects of their behaviours. After all, when you're in control, you tend to be getting your way, and there's less emphasis on any negative bits. It's as if CFs ignore all the crap that gets stirred up as a result of their behaviours, reframing situations to put a positive spin on the way they've handled things, even patting themselves on the back for delivering their objectives, and usually disregarding the consequences for those around them. Imagine then how difficult it is to influence a CF to even consider making the smallest behavioural changes, when they're completely blinkered to the negatives.

The CF Stigma

Most CFs are unaware that controlling behaviours can cause a huge blemish on your reputation – a kind of social disgrace that has people disinclined to want to buddy up and hang out with you. Because the focus is on the benefits of controlling outcomes, CFs are pretty much oblivious to the reasons why they're often left out in the cold. It's the mark of the CF – a stigma so profound that it literally drives people away.

Looking back, people's responses to my controlling behaviours were mostly subtle and confusing. A few friends and partners moved slowly away over time, leaving me with a bunch of 'why' questions. Some chose to distance themselves because they simply couldn't muster the courage to tell me straight out what annoyed them so much about me. Many a CF would say these people were gutless. The fact is, at the time, I just wasn't the kind of person they felt they could have fronted up to with such a declaration. They were just too uneasy about discussing this issue outright, fearing what my reaction might be.

Years later, after a lengthy stretch of soul-searching, I finally began to understand why the prospect of tackling me head on would have been so daunting. I began to realise that it wasn't necessarily fear that made them turn and walk away; it was something about my character that made these people I loved unwilling to open up their hearts and share what was there. When I finally understood how my behaviours had been affecting people dear to me, I knew the time for me to lighten up and drop the control reins was way overdue. If it had been just one or two people that had walked out of my life, I could have comfortably waved it off as a result of flaws in their character. But after it had occurred several times with those nearest and dearest, it would have been foolish not to start asking myself some tough questions about what it's truly like for others to try to relate to me. Unrelenting in my search for answers, I did ask more than a few hard-line questions of myself and others, landing responses that were both confronting and insightful. I eventually came to know what it was like for those on the receiving end of my controlling behaviours. Not a pretty picture!

Feeling the Impacts

Simply reading or talking about the negatives of CF behaviour won't necessarily translate into experiential learnings. There's a need to *feel* what the impacts are – taking on all that it means on a personal level. As an extension of the dis-advantages already outlined, here are a few not-so-nice impacts of being a CF. In other words, how it's going to affect *you* personally. Here's hoping these ring some alarm bells:

- Friends/partners can disappear from your life without ever telling you why – "I just couldn't breathe anymore within his tight, controlled little world".

- You may not be that welcome at group social events – "Don't invite her – we want a fun, spontaneous night, don't we?"

- People may have a (really) hard time trying to get to know the real you – "I only ever get to see the person he wants me to see".

- You never/rarely get to access your vulnerable side and those close to you don't get to see it – "I love his soft, gentle side, but he hardly ever shows it. I feel shut out".

- People may be reluctant to reveal their preferences, because they know you're going to take over anyway – "Why bother telling her what I want? She always ends up getting her own way."

- You're seen as uptight and demanding – "If only he'd let go of his need for things to be a certain way, he'd be so much easier to be around".

- You may not get to hear what people really think or feel – "Why would I tell her how I feel? She wouldn't be open to hearing what I say anyway".

Reading these words, knowing people close to you could be saying more-or-less the same things, may help you register something emotionally. The impact that controlling tendencies have on your life needs to be *felt,* not in-your-head analysed. It's only in feeling the impact that we develop a deep comprehension of what's playing out in our interactions with others. Sure, it can be unpleasant, if not downright distressing, to hear or know that someone you love, respect or value may be feeling this way about their relationship with you. But at some time you need to acknowledge the awful truth, and really let it hit home how your behaviours are affecting your life and the lives of those closest to you. Be prepared though – this is bound to send massive shock waves through your system.

"He never listens to our feelings!"

Making Mountains Out of Molehills

There's an even bigger 'metaphysical' downside here. If you believe in the law of attraction – the principle that like attracts like – there are grave repercussions from constantly being on the lookout for what could go wrong (as happens with CF hyper-vigilance). Not only is the majority of our focus zoning in on all the troublesome stuff, filling our minds and lives with rubbishy unpleasantness; but also this negative fixation spawns further low-grade thoughts, which all collect to manifest a truly disagreeable existence. Simply put, negative mind fodder breeds relentlessly. Now, if you're someone who revels in the masochistic lifestyle, best of luck to you. But if you don't get off on feeding your own suffering (or have had more than enough of doing so), and you'd prefer not to live a life filled with gloomy forecasting, best to nip any hint of hyper-vigilance in the bud. When you're preoccupied with fear-based negative thoughts, there's just not the mind space for much else, definitely not happy, positive, friendly thoughts.

Closely related to the law of attraction is the insight 'what you resist persists'[5], which makes a whole lot of sense. If you're intent on making sure something doesn't happen or you're focused on something terrible that's popped up in your life, much of your energy and attention will be pouring into that. In a sense, you magnify the negative experience by thinking it into becoming something a whole lot bigger than it actually is. So much time and effort is spent in resisting what is, it starts consuming us, and we end up finding it near impossible to let go. The same thing applies to any of the negatives we focus on in life. Resistance requires energy. Any energy we channel into battling perceived negativities is not only self-disabling, it also cripples our capacity for taking action to empower our lives. Instead of focusing our energies on wrestling unwanted occurrences, we need to redirect our energies to focus on positive alternatives: love over hate/discord; wealth over poverty; opportunities over 'what's missing'.

Takeaway: whatever we keep our focus on increases the likelihood of it manifesting.

Flipside – Impacts on Others

CFs can be oh so sensitive to feeling we're being controlled, yet we don't always see how our own behaviours impact on others. It's typical 'look in the mirror' stuff – projecting onto others the behaviours we display ourselves, but usually can't see or tolerate. Until we actually take on board the notion that we may indeed have controlling tendencies, they're almost impossible to catch in the act. So we keep thinking all the nasty behaviours are 'out there' and not 'in here' – yet another delusion and a good way of deflecting responsibility for our behaviours away from ourselves. The catch here is, if we're not open to taking on responsibility for our actions, there's no way we'll be ready or able to see how they impact on others.

Much of the time, CFs can be cut-off from acknowledging the feelings of others (to say nothing of being disconnected to our own feelings), unless, of course, it has some direct or indirect personal benefit. Here's where controlling behaviours overlap with narcissism – it's all about "What's in it for me?" Careless disregard for how our actions affect others can border, at times, on anti-social behaviour. The emotional connection's just not there. CFs can lack empathy and understanding and often couldn't give two hoots if someone experiences grief, as long as we're not negatively impacted in any way, shape or form.

Sounds harsh? Well, some CFs are a lot more uncaring and oblivious to their surroundings than others. But the reality here is that all CF attempts at control are fundamentally based on a need to keep their fears at bay and anxiety in check. Think of it as a survival instinct – we only do this because every situation where the result is unpredictable is seen as one that could potentially threaten our survival. Now imagine living through this lens of fear (if you're not a CF who already knows they do). From that place, it's pretty difficult to think you'd have the wherewithal to act with others' feelings in mind.

Being on the receiving end of CF behaviours definitely has a huge downside. How much damage the impacts have is almost purely dependent on the recipient's level of self-awareness and understanding. If someone has a reasonably solid level of self-worth and assertiveness, the effects of being at the pointy end of controlling behaviour will be a lot less than on someone who suffers low self-worth and clings hopelessly to the CF for some kind of self-validation. Those with a more stable self-identity probably wouldn't be seen associating with a dictatorial-type CF too often anyway – they just wouldn't bother putting up with any of their 'shit' (read: disrespectful behaviours).

Here are just a few examples of how controlling behaviours can impact others (brace yourself). When spending time around a CF, chances are people will feel:

- Bossed and bullied – this happens when people are verbally and emotionally abused and manipulated. Something CFs may not even recognise they do.
- Unable to communicate effectively – CFs have trouble listening and so don't always hear what other people have to say. It's almost as if what they do have to say just isn't valuable.
- Belittled, incompetent, patronised, inferior – CFs honestly believe no one can do things as well as they can, and they have no hesitation in pointing that out to others.
- Like they have to walk on eggshells – CFs are likely to blow up, completely shut down or worse, if people don't do things the way they want them done.
- Extremely self-conscious – over time, being around a CF really takes its toll, and others can start thinking the problem may very well be theirs, which of course it isn't.

- As if nothing they do, say or give is ever going to be good enough – because for a CF it isn't, is it? Even when they do get it right, the CF may decide to change the playing field.

- Suffocated and trapped by domineering behaviours – CFs tell others what they should do, say and act, when and where, offering advice even when it's not asked for.

- Anxious, stressed out, on edge, perhaps even scared – people need almost superhuman levels of patience, tolerance and understanding to be in a close relationship with a CF.

- Like they can't be themselves – CFs are always dictating how and who they should be. There's rarely any room for individual decisions and opinions to come alive.

- Exhausted, sick and tired of the CFs overbearing nature – and probably ready to walk.

Doesn't sound very nice, does it? Reading through the list, it's not so hard to imagine what it's like to be on the receiving end of CF behaviours. Hackles used to go up on the back of my neck when I was on the receiving end of CF manipulation. It was like, "Back off bud, you don't have a chance of walking over me". A more-than-reasonably-required defensiveness flared up. Like a standoff, I sensed I was being challenged, and my competitive, fired-up CF came out ready for a fight. Some major buttons were being pressed. Most, but not all, of the time I could compose an appropriate response, even force myself to produce a smile. But when I couldn't, I felt like going in for the 'kill' (ggrrrrrr!). Not a good look. Nowadays, I can see a CF challenge for what it is – someone's fearful insecurities at play – and I'm able to step back and watch it play out with my boundaries firmly in place. Well... most of the time!

And so I look back now on those that fell prey to my CF behaviours with understanding and big chunks of empathy, lamenting how different things could have been...

SEVEN

CF SPOTTING OPPORTUNITIES

W e're nearing the end of Part One, and at this point you've probably figured out whether you (or someone you know) are a CF. Now, this realisation should never be taken lightly. Not only can it kick off a self-enquiry process that promises to radically transform the way you interact with the world, it can also assist you in identifying both common and more unusual CF-centric circumstances.

Staying alert, but not alarmed, could literally save your butt if you look out for potentially volatile CF situations. Here, it's wise to observe and refrain from participation, even if you're busting to jump on in. If you notice one on the build or already in play, and you're not directly affected, just sit back and feast your eyes on the action. If you're a CF caught in one of these scenarios, see if you can generate even a smidgen of self-awareness to save yourself some of the inevitable embarrassment bound to occur afterwards.

So, here they are, some interesting CF watching opportunities:

- ***The CF Status Competition.*** Competing CFs will often pull out a no-holds-barred approach to winning, involving lies, trickery, and unfair play, as they battle for status supremacy. Observers may be perplexed by the manic rivalry and obsessive conduct on display. These situations have the potential to escalate into extreme hostility. Best to keep your distance.

- ***The CF vs. CF Standoff.*** A highly volatile situation, especially when power or reputation is involved (and they nearly always are). When a stand-off occurs between two CFs, viciousness can erupt that has the potential to end in public humiliation, loss of employment, destroyed relationships, or other life-changing dilemmas. Stay well out of their line of sight.

- ***Mutiny Against the CF.*** This typically occurs in work situations, but can also occur in friend networks and family groups. Usually a consequence of the CF victim/s having reached a breaking point in bearing the brunt of hardcore CF behaviours over time. Mutinies may result in the CF having no friends, family or allies. On occasion, the CF may lash out, sometimes aggressively, against the perceived perpetrators, attempting to bully or shame them into submission. If pre-planned, best hope someone hired a security guard in case any worst-case scenarios unfold.

- ***The (Almost) Impotent CF.*** A disagreement with a once powerful CF, who's now on the verge of being defunct. Extreme self-care is required here, as these individuals have nothing to lose, and could push those around them into therapy or early-onset senility.

- ***CF Abandonment.*** This typically occurs in intimate relationships when the CF is unwilling or unprepared to face up to the impacts of their behaviours, and their partner decides enough is enough. Extreme emotional triggering could result in dangerous CF reactions that should be anticipated and prepared for well in advance. Be at the ready to phone-a-friend or dial emergency.

"Courage, Miss Tessmacher—when I make a break for the water cooler, you lead the staff out by the fire stairs."

PART TWO

"Knowing others is intelligence;

knowing yourself is true wisdom.

Mastering others is strength;

mastering yourself is true power."

Lao Tzu

You've now arrived at a crossroads. I'll assume that by this point you've diligently read Part One, and now know more than the basics about what controlling behaviours are all about. Some of you may have even started applying this info to you and your life. But these learnings as a standalone are pretty much useless – unapplied knowledge rarely gets us anywhere, unless it's utilised to improve our particular situation and self-awareness develops as a result. Meaning unless you get to know more about how you think, feel and operate, it's merely another piece of wasted advice.

In Part Two, we'll look into how we can manage our behaviours more effectively, so we don't push others away (or over the edge) and we don't mess up what's important to us in life. We'll delve a little deeper into how it feels to live from a CF perspective, how our expectations cause us all kinds of problems, how we can reframe uncertainty so it excites us (instead of scaring the living daylights out of us), and how we can start relaxing into the present moment, building self-awareness and acceptance along the way.

So let's get going...

(EIGHT)

BREAK ON THROUGH

"The best way out is always through."

Robert Frost

Saddle Up for the Ride of Your Life

First off, any decision regarding a major life rethink or personality detour demands we take a long hard look at where we are right now. There's no way we can intentionally make a change, moving from here to where we want to be, unless we're very clear about our starting point. We'd be clueless; not knowing how far we'd progressed or in which direction. Knowing where you are now – your beliefs, behaviours and characteristics – is absolutely essential if you're truly serious about changing things that just aren't working for you. Add to this an in-depth assessment of the results currently showing up in your life based on your CF nature – in love, work and play – and the 'how it is' picture you paint (assuming you've been brutally honest) should hopefully be enough to spur you into action. Openness and willingness are the key ingredients here. By making the effort to understand where you're at, and being more than a tad curious to find out how you tick, you're bound to be able to make the changes you want. Even it if does take some time to figure out exactly how to go about it.

When standing at my own crossroads, it became startlingly obvious just how much of an enormous impact my CF self was having. It was undeniable; my behaviours bordered on being ruinous at times, and I knew I needed to stop being that way if I wanted any kind of long-term fulfilment. Looking back, I jotted down all the consequences my controlling had had over the years (well, as much as I could remember), then started probing my memories for answers as to why I'd felt the need to act that way at the time. Taking closer notice of my behaviours also helped me become aware of trigger points that initiated my need to control or influence a person or outcome, enabling me to dig up the thoughts, beliefs and fears simmering away in my subconscious. Over time, I built up plenty of knowledge of and awareness about how I operated in the world. Not comforting stuff to wake up to, but way better than living in the dark and having the wrong kind of results turning up in my life. I eventually reached a point where I was more than ready to accept things could be different, in a better way, and that I needed to get to it and make some changes. Sure enough, I had heaps of work to do.

Hopeful, but more than a bit doubtful of my ability to change, I pushed myself headfirst into a personality metamorphosis. Shortly after starting the process, it felt like one step forward, two steps back. For quite a while, probably because of an inherent resistance to such a change, I felt I was getting nowhere, even losing ground. All of my crap came to the surface, and it was difficult to look at it, let alone own it and deal with it. Other times, I had some amazing insights and breakthroughs that propelled my eagerness to know more and keep pursuing the work I'd begun. Still, with my awareness training wheels on, I didn't always notice the changes. Others did, and they let me know in no uncertain terms I was on the right track and better not stray off course. I couldn't turn back at that point, even if I wanted to. A ripening self-awareness called on me to finally stand and face my demons, refusing to let me escape by reverting to my old ways of being. The only path open to me faced forward.

Smashing the Veneer

From square one, what became remarkably apparent was this: even though I conveyed a confident, gutsy persona to the world, many of my behaviours were driven by massive insecurities. Fears had engulfed my life, falsely promising to protect, but instead suffocating the freedom, creativity and aliveness that ached for expression. My personality acted like a camouflage, covering over my fears and insecurities with a bravado that fooled many, myself included. This illusory veneer projected an image of super-confidence, quirky optimism, and first-rate competence. The controlling behaviours supporting this facade convinced me I was more than highly capable of making my life safer and more predictable by being the designated driver on the course of any event featured in my life.

That was the illusion I'd been living with – not only could I control the world I lived in to get the outcomes I needed, but I was also by far the best person to manipulate everything in order to get there. Terrified of not knowing what was around the corner, I'd do my very best to make sure life was predictable by controlling here, there and everywhere I could. The insanity of it all was that sometimes I caused the very thing I feared most. Driven by what bordered on sheer paranoia that something horrible could happen and pain was virtually imminent (a couple of relationship breakups come to mind here), I eventually caused that very outcome to occur. Because I couldn't stand the unbearable possibility that someone or something else would cause it, leaving me completely unprepared and vulnerable, I made sure I called the shots. With a compelling need to keep things predictable, I manifested the outcomes I feared most, and in an odd way felt comfortably in control of the situation. Weird, huh?

As I moved deeper into peeling back the layers of my CF issues, it became clear I'd eventually need to smash this veneer and reveal my real self for all to see, imperfections and all – a hugely nerve-wracking feeling. Knowing I'd probably prefer to dance naked in front of a group of outback miners who hadn't seen a woman for a year, I prepared to ready myself and gradually work up to that future disrobing. By divulging my flaws and weaknesses little by little to those closest to me, and feeling more and more appreciated and supported in that process, I moved past my initial feeling of being completely exposed and unprotected. Over time, while I still felt a (sometimes humungous) vulnerability without my veneer, I came to realise that not only was I able to connect with people in a more authentic way, but that they loved me 'warts and all' – I was more than 'good enough', even with all my insecurities and idiosyncrasies on full display.

In her romantic life, Susan always managed
to seize defeat from the jaws of victory.

Taming the Monkey Mind

Before opening to up to the journey of self-discovery, most of my energy went into thinking about how to control externalities, keeping the surface calm and steady, and hardly any time was spent connecting with self. I'd never even contemplated the idea of opening up to my fears, and delving into the feelings behind them was more than a little overwhelming. Squash 'em down, keep 'em hidden was my unspoken motto. There was no comfort or sense in checking in, only to find my mind running wild with fearful thoughts. I'd written 'meditate' on my daily 'To Do' list for years, yet rarely exercised the motivation or self-discipline needed to be still enough for a time so I could tick it off. It was so much easier to believe that someone 'out there' was the cause of any dilemma I found myself in – certainly helped with deflecting responsibility. Reasoning that I could get on with the task of looking within and stilling my mind if things would only settle down in my external world, I begged off meditation and other forms of navel gazing, always waiting for a better time to come along.

Intrinsic to the change process was the unstated demand – you will get to know yourself, no matter how uncomfortable or tedious the process. So when I eventually did sit down to quietness, cultivating the minimal amount of willpower needed to still my thoughts (even that was an effort), I found a mind running amok that had literally hijacked my life. All these what-happens-if scenarios played out repeatedly, causing an almost constant state of background anxiety I'd managed to conceal from the world, remaining relatively impervious to it myself. While all this effort had been exerted trying to control others, the untamed beast within, the source of my feeling the need for certainty and control over everything in the first place, had been completely overlooked. It was a monkey mind – restless, confused, mischievous, and undoubtedly out of control.

> *"A ruffled mind makes a restless pillow."*

> Charlotte Bronte

Wise comments over the years from well-intentioned friends suggested time and again that I 'get out of my head'. Being the queen of analytical thinking and not being able to grasp a different way of being, I really struggled to work out what that meant. It took quite a while for me to understand that not everything needs in-your-head analysing and assessing, which was the basis I'd operated on my entire life. Eventually I relented, taking the advice on board, and finally became willing enough to have a look at what this feeling stuff was all about, and if it could be of any help whatsoever.

What I discovered was that I was so 'in my head', I really had no idea what was happening to this body of mine I depended on so much. Tuning in to the physical, I felt a body starved for attention and care. I'd driven it so hard over the years, engaged in athletic pursuits (as a way of trying to prove my worthiness), my muscles now ached almost constantly. Tuning in to my emotions, I sensed huge amounts of anger, frustration and grief – things I'd strived to bury and control along with everything else. When the reality of 'what is' hit home, it was more than a little overwhelming. With so many issues to address, I asked myself over and again "Can I really turn all this around? If it is possible, where on earth do I begin?"

Figuring that beginning with whatever came up was as good a place as any for a starting point, I learned to catch my behaviours, even thoughts, as they unfolded. Like a cat standing ready to pounce on its prey, I became more and more adept at watching out and leaping all over my own stuff. Latching onto actions and mannerisms that seemed a bit off in terms of intention or delivery, I identified heaps of things that were sure to have rubbed people the wrong way. And whenever I did pick up on something, I foraged around to find out what prompted me to act or respond in that manner. That was the tough piece – practicing watching yourself more-or-less objectively (as much as you possibly can), and then entering a no-nonsense enquiry to locate the triggered emotion underneath that behaviour. It takes lots of practice, developing a keen sense of self-awareness so you know what kind of messages ignite what kind of emotional reactions in you. I never said this was going to be easy, but if you have the patience and persistence, and are fully committed to knowing the full, unadulterated version of you, it can definitely be done.

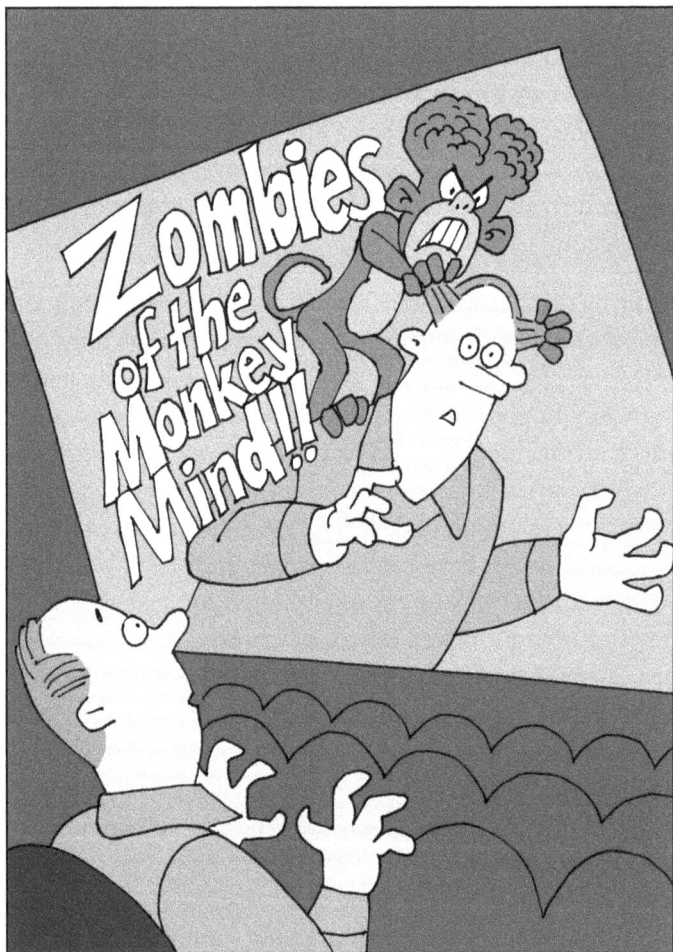

He knew it was just a grade-Z movie, but Jerry still felt
something oddly familiar about it.

Taking Back the Reins

As I kept at it, working at tuning in and building self-knowledge, a softer side of me started to unfold, replacing the dictatorial manner I'd carried around for decades. All the feeling stuff was pretty much foreign to me before this; in my head, feelings were so closely associated with emotions that experiencing them signalled weakness and an inability to control whatever was going on inside. They had always been something to avoid, repress, or control if they did come to the surface. Now though, my feelings began to get the time they needed to express themselves appropriately, instead of blurting out uncontrollably at the most inappropriate of times or for manipulative reasons. When I finally allowed myself the time and space to be still, I was able to access raw emotions that before I'd only noticed erupting under pressure-cooker conditions. This newly-developed skill enabled me to feel feelings accompanied by a self-control that wasn't rigid, but supportive of my best interests. It enabled me to get to know the real me – not the veneer I showed the world and had bought into myself.

The process of change seriously accelerated when I first acknowledged, then started to accept, a core part of myself I'd long ago given away control over. As far back as I can remember, the self-protector part of me had fended off anything perceived as potentially dangerous, whether from interpersonal relations or life circumstances. It had served me well in the past when I was too young or a lot less able to take care of myself (read: emotionally immature). Now I realised the time had come to wrestle back control from my self-protector, so I could finally start being fully responsible for my life and become unrestricted by unreasonable fears.

To do that, I first acknowledged the role my self-protector had played in my life to date and the benefits which had flowed from that. I learned quickly that it wasn't sensible to run riot and try to force it out of existence – it would just rear up and sabotage any effort I made. The trick was in getting to know why my self-protector was there, understanding its motives, tactics and reasoning. The next step was to access other parts of me (yes, we all have parts within us) that were prepared and able to take over the role of directing my life from a more relaxed, less fearful perspective. Then gradually, and I mean gradually, nudging those more functional parts in to take the reins.

It's important to note that the change process doesn't have an expiry date. There's always something to learn; stretching and growing myself here and there keeps me on my toes. There are times I find myself getting lazy and falling back into a few old mind and behavioural habits. But just like fitness or weight loss, you know what needs to be done to get back in shape. So I retrain myself to take back the reins once more. Because the focus is on self-development, it's expanded way beyond a purely CF focus to encapsulate many other aspects of my life, which may or may not have interlaced with those initial controlling behaviours.

One should always be vigilant with the monkey mind – you think you've got one thing down pat and the next issue comes up for a bite. Mastering the mind is the greatest quest we can undertake – one that's extremely demanding but loaded with rewards. It makes life so much more interesting. But for many of us, the change just seems too difficult to undertake…

Digging Your Heels In

Deny! Deny! Deny! That's pretty much the result when a CF first comes face-to-face with the possibility (or what others might call 'undeniable fact') that controlling behaviours define a big part of how they come across in the world. And for some, denial is the place they're quite content to stay. Talk about stubborn – these CFs refuse to see the negative impacts of their behaviours, even when their wife/husband/partner/friend tells them over and over again and then walks out of their lives for good. They live in such a tight little box, hounded by insecurities left, right and centre, and the thought of facing (even acknowledging) their fears and making even the smallest change is simply beyond comprehension. With a tenuous grip on coping with life, they need to keep things just as they are so they feel capable of surviving this world. Unfortunately, there's no point in trying to get a CF to see the light if they're up to their ears in denial. They'll do what they do in their own time.

Many of us move past the denial stage, but get stuck in the "Okay, so what if I am a CF?" stage. We start defending ourselves, even arguing in favour of our CF tendencies – "Well, at least I'm in control of my life". Rationalising that it can't be too terrible, because we wouldn't have got to where we are today without being this way, we dig our heels in and fire off at anyone who dares to persuade us it's time to change.

**"Change? Me? I like who I am.
It serves me being this way."**

At this point, it can be hugely difficult to see and accept the negative side of our controlling behaviours. With our blinkers on to how everyone else is experiencing us, we only see the up side – getting our way most of the time. We're stuck between denial and acknowledgement – realising that we do have these controlling behaviours, but not quite ready to face the hard facts and feelings of how they play a detrimental role in our everyday lives. Stuck in this mind-set, we're not quite ready for change – the incentive just isn't attractive enough for us to jump on the change wagon. Think about it... how many people do you know who are seriously committed to examining their lives and making the required changes? There aren't too many out there. Why? Two core reasons:

1. Most of us are pretty much used to identifying with the personality we've had for all these years – so the thought of changing who we are isn't at all appealing as it affects

our very identity to a greater or lesser degree. There's got to be a pretty good understanding of the need for change and a compelling sense of urgency to undertake it; and

2. It's incredibly difficult to muster the energy and resilience to make a profound self-transformation, much less stick out the course once it's started.

Let's go into a little more detail...

NINE

RESISTING THE CHANGE WE NEED

E ven if we get to a place where we understand there's an issue to resolve and something needs to be done to remedy it, our resistance demons can still step in and argue for keeping the status quo intact. There are loads of reasons why nervousness or anxiety shows up when we're faced with change. Typically for CFs, change is viewed as a frightening process involving an uncertainty which clouds any clarity around an end result. It's the ambiguity, this un- known element we can't predict, that's inevitably challeng- ing for those with control issues. As CFs, we suffer major re- sistance to what we don't know or can't determine out there (externally), imagine how nerve-wracking it is to contem- plate changes in here (internally), particularly when there's so much disconnection to what's within.

When our change resistor is out in full force, the motivating influence is one of these goodies:

a. We don't understand or have enough evidence there's a problem

When we're stuck in a state of deep denial about being a CF, or haven't yet acknowledged the full impact of our controlling behaviours, it's difficult to see a reason for change. CFs are uncomfortably comfortable in putting up with the down sides associated with their behaviour – that is, if their blinkers don't stop them from ignoring it altogether.

Some of the more obstinate ones continue to deny and refute the obvious fact they're a CF, no matter how much proof is tabled as evidence of their controlling ways. Again and again, the CF in the denial or 'so what' stage will cite personality differences, other people's ignorance, even envy as reasons behind the 'proof' presented in the first place. When people close to them let them know in no uncertain terms just how controlling they are over and over again, these CFs refuse to see their behaviours as problematic and in desperate need of being addressed. They're just not ready to see it.

Certainly, in the height of my CF days, the comments and evidence I was presented with supported my theory that all the 'others' had a problem in not being able to accept who I was (lack of acceptance being a repetitive theme through my life). My sincere belief was that people were judging me for simply being different and in control of my life. In hindsight, I can see at the time I wasn't ready to face up to this shadowy side of my personality. I *seemed* to be doing such a great job of holding everything together and getting things done, so I just wasn't interested in taking in any feedback which might contradict that. Of course, to have been willing to assimilate the feedback would've required me to start taking responsibility for my behaviours and exercising some self-control. What a strange and unfamiliar concept!

Tips for acknowledging there's an issue:

➢ Ask friends and family members (ones that won't dance around the subject) if you have controlling behaviours and how they might be impacting your life.

➢ Reread the sections regarding the impacts of being a CF (Chapter Six), then ask yourself, "If I do have an issue with controlling, how could that be affecting my life and what could I do about it?"

➢ Do your own reality check – if you've got the guts to. Be a scientist of sorts and try to disprove the theory that you are a CF.

In spite of the evidence, Gail remained steadfast
that her point-of-view was the correct one.

b. We're unconvinced of the benefits of changing

Many of us are exceptionally attached to the way we are and can't see the sense in changing. Even if our personality traits occasionally make us cringe or get people offside, we've grown accustomed over the years to the ebb and flow of it all. Some even loathe (pretty harsh) the way they are, finding it hard to spot any of their positive points, but still balk at the mention of making profound character changes. We become creatures of habit – some good, some not so good!

When we're comfortable with the way things are, even if it's sometimes an uncomfortable comfortableness, it's less likely we'll be inclined to look seriously at the benefits change could bring. If this is the case, any benefits associated with making change would probably be considered to provide less of an advantage than the benefits we believe we're gaining from our existing behaviours. We'd undoubtedly be pretty darn good at convincing ourselves absolutely that there are few if any benefits associated with changing our controlling behaviours. Why fix something that seems to work well most of the time? Put simply, from this vantage point the benefits of change just don't look like they'll ever outweigh the disadvantages. With this belief, why would you ever bother putting yourself through the potential turmoil of transformation?

This form of resistance relates strongly to another concern (which is not restricted to CFs) – that the outcomes of change are unknown. You can commit to changing yourself, start the process, become uncomfortable as you churn through it, notice small changes, but still have no clear idea what the end results might look like. You just don't know where you'll end up or who you'll turn out to be. The process requires a degree of faith – you put in the work to build your self-awareness and alter dysfunctional behaviours with the hope (and expectation) that your effort will bear the right kind of fruit (think tasty strawberries not stinky durians). By loosening your grip to a greater or lesser degree, and trusting in yourself and the process of change, life will inevitably start flowing more easily. Most CFs consider such transformational change a frightening experience (akin to a rollercoaster ride) compared to sitting comfortably in the control seat for numerous years. And it will be if you scream your lungs out for the whole ride. Best to relax into it, watch how your fears respond to the situation (knowing *you* are not your fears), and hang on for the ride of your life.

Due to the many elements of unpredictability, we CFs aren't so quick to jump on board the change wagon full of enthusiasm and glee. At times, it may seem more sensible to stay with the devil you know. I mean, why risk it all for something that sounds beneficial on paper, but requires a shift so profound that it will fundamentally alter your personality and how people perceive you? Change itself is fluid, unpredictable and predominantly intangible – the antithesis of the predictability and stability we CFs strive for. An appetite for change, whether relating to specific situations, with particular people, or personal change, is not a natural state for CFs. It's an odd, out-of-the-box notion that's viewed as nonsensical, if not downright offensive or even dangerous in certain circumstances. When a push towards change is attempted by an external party and has not been initiated by the CF personally, it will surely be ill received and will inevitably be challenged or rejected outright. For change of this type to be seriously considered, CFs really need to cotton on to the benefits at a very personal level.

Tips for seeing the benefits of change:

➢ Start getting real about the disadvantages of being a CF – write a list of how your CF behaviours may be affecting different areas of your life (refer back to Chapter Six). And if you really don't know, sit down with a couple of friends and let them fill you in.

➢ While you're at it, ask those same friends what benefits they see in you taking on a self-change challenge. Perhaps jot down a few pointers.

➢ Write another list that details the types of outcomes you could shoot for – ones that would be hugely advantageous if you pursued personal change.

c. We feel we aren't capable or don't have the resources needed for change

Akin to thinking, "I'm an old dog, and these are definitely new tricks", many people convince themselves they simply aren't capable of changing. In real terms, they're just exchanging an unwillingness to change for an inability to change. In other words, it's just an excuse. We're all capable of change, even the most stubborn amongst us. This is most evident when we have change unexpectedly thrust upon us. We might grizzle, gripe and go into the doldrums for a while, but the vast majority of the time, we can adapt and do. Even if we feel we're being dragged kicking and screaming.

Along similar lines, you may feel you lack the resources required to support yourself through change of this magnitude. That doesn't mean you can't go out there and gather up that support – be resourceful. If it's internal support you feel a shortage of, look into what specifically you feel is needed in order to make the required changes. Acknowledge this concern as a natural ego-based fear that's trying to inhibit you from making any significant changes. And remember, you're not your ego (a rather metaphysical concept, I know), so you can change despite its persistent protests and any fears it may throw in your way.

It's important to note that when we're not ready to take on a big challenge, even one that offers the potential to deliver huge benefits, our typical default is to make excuses (to ourselves and others) for not undertaking it. If it's change that alters our way of being and realigns our worldview, we've got to expect at least some internal pushback in the guise of excuses and resistance. Most of the time it's simply a matter of seeing through the excuses to the fears propping them up and then addressing those fears.

Tips on feeling supported:

➢ Don't just sit there playing around with a victim or 'poor me' attitude. Make a list of what resources (internal and external) you might need. Then go forth and seek them out.

➢ Speak with friends and family about the change you're looking to take on, and request some support – be specific about what it is you need from them (refer back to your list).

➢ Remember, the first step is a powerful commitment to change. Don't leave it for some time in the future, act now with small steps. This affirms your commitment to change.

➢ Ultimately, you are the greatest source of support for yourself. Be your own cheerleader!

The vast wall had been built to keep everyone out, and Stanley knew it would be a gargantuan task to dismantle it. But at least he had the right tools for the job.

d. We're just not interested in or have an aversion to the change

When we start to consider taking on this type of personal change, our sub-conscious fears are stirred up, and our self-protector rises predictably to the occasion in an attempt to fend off any changes to the status quo. It'll use every excuse, cast doubt on every option, throw accusations here and there, and introduce unanticipated obstacles, all with the sole purpose of turning us away from the path of change and maintaining the dysfunctional equilibrium of our present state.

So if you're totally disinterested in changing your (supposed) controlling behaviours, take a good look behind that disinterest. You'll probably find there's something lurking in the background that may sound like a legitimate reason not to change, but flags itself as more of a giant cop-out excuse to those in the know around you. By taking a closer, more objective look at your justifications, you might just see what everyone else does.

Note that sometimes, there are other, more valid, excuses for deciding to forego change at the present time; other goals or focus points we deem more of a priority for us to take on or deal with at this point. We may be struggling to fit into a new work environment, coping with a sick parent or child, or dealing with significant health issues. While these could be seen as excuses, they can also be genuine issues, and I'm not one to condone beating yourself up by lumping even more stress on your plate. If this really is the situation you find yourself in, defer the change for now, but remember to revisit it again when things have settled down.

There will always be people who, no matter how problematic their issue is or how dire the consequences of their inaction, just don't want to take the path to change. They haven't reached the "Holy crap, look at how this is affecting my life" stage of acknowledgement. They're stuck in the "Don't know; don't care; okay with how it is" stage. Inside, there could be some major alarm bells going off, but you wouldn't know it from the outside. They often adopt a kind of stoic reserve or righteous indignation (both forms of self-protection) when someone confronts them, keenly guarding their right of choice. People in this state are terrified, and their terror freezes them into a state of helpless inaction where they remain uncomfortably comfortable. Unfortunately, no amount of rationalising, bribing or coercion will be enough to encourage these CFs to change at this time. Often these people need urgent assistance and support to change, but sadly turn away when it's offered.

Tips for moving through inner resistance or aversion to change:

➢ Check in with a partner or friend and discuss your reasons for not wanting to make personal changes at this time, then ask for their honest feedback (remember to do that last bit).

➢ By far the single most important thing you can do is to acknowledge any fears you may have around change. To do this you need to allocate some uninterrupted time by yourself. When alone, preferably in quiet surroundings, sit down comfortably, relax your body and ease your mind. Then contemplate the change – visualise approaching the change and feel the sensations that arise in your body (many people experience a sensation like butterflies in the belly or certain muscles tensing). Notice what's there; don't try and fix it or analyse your way out of it. Stay in this position and be with the feelings for 10-15 minutes, then write down what came up for you (preferably in a personal journal). By learning to acknowledge and face our fears, we start taking back the power they've had over us.

➢ If you're really up for a new experience, once you've noticed the bodily sensations relating to the fear of change, try asking your body what it fears most (that's right, speak to the parts of your body where you feel the sensations). You don't have to do this aloud, and it will not render you insane. Just listen to the response – it may be words that pop into your head, a feeling that arises, or even images that come to mind. Write down your experience and anything else that flows from that.

Fluffy Stuff Behind the Control

When we come across some new piece of information about ourselves, something we're actually prepared to consider and not scoff at willy-nilly and dismiss right off the bat, we want to analyse, rationalise and test it, turning it upside down and around in our heads to see if it fits. Once it passes the initial checkpoint, our reasoning minds are eager to grab hold of it, trying somehow to assimilate it into the current notions we have of ourselves. If it's information that's somewhat confronting (like finding out you may very well be a CF), the mind can end up doing cartwheels while deciding whether or not to integrate this knowledge and how to do it in a way that minimises anxiety and distress. If the new info is stamped as a reject and fails to get integrated, we can easily fall into denial and resist any suggested change. If integration is successful to a greater or lesser degree, we typically move into the 'so what' stage, before heading on over to start the actual change process. Moving beyond the 'so what' stage requires an approach that's sure to be quite foreign, and more than a little disturbing, for the vast majority of CFs out there.

So we've got this info about ourselves, and we keep on milling it around in our minds – finding examples to back it up or refute it, wondering why we act in weird ways at times, and thinking how this might change EVERYTHING if we do decide to act on it. The problem here is that analysing a confronting issue to the nth degree doesn't get us very far in terms of initiating any kind of personal change. CFs like to think it does (they're putting so much effort into it after all), but like an old vinyl record caught on a scratch, replaying the same line over and again, ruminating over this can create a continual loop process which fails to get us close to the heart of the matter. Put another way – I can analyse a facet of my personality till the cows come home; it may help me to understand myself a lot better, but in no way does it give me the incentive to transform those behaviours. Where we're really going to get the "Oh crap" effect we need in order to motivate ourselves to change is by *feeling* what it's like to be a CF (we touched on this earlier in Chapter Six). It's through our feelings that we connect with the impact our behaviours have on others and ourselves.

For many, that's easier said than done. Thing is, the majority of us have an enormous challenge getting in touch with our feelings. In our Western society, knowledge, intellect and reason are highly valued. The head predominates over the heart in so many things we do – even love and romance (go figure). We're taught from an early age (especially boys) that showing feelings equates with weakness (though I hear this may slowly be shifting). So we bottle up all of our feelings of rejection, jealousy, abandonment, loneliness, envy, helplessness, hopelessness and failure, shoving them deep down where it's so much harder to access them. Instead of being allowed a natural expression, our feelings seep out through our words and behaviours, even manifesting in massive amounts of stress, as we do our very best to put on a strong face and be 'appropriate', 'good enough', and 'in control' in the public eye.

What we commonly don't or won't acknowledge is the power of our feelings and the courage it takes to tap into them. That's because we've become completely disengaged with this fundamental part of who we are. Feelings and emotions are often viewed as wild and untameable – hard to get a handle on, let alone become comfortable with. Yet feelings are the channel through which we connect with our reality within. They're the secret key that opens us up to an entirely mysterious inner world. Only when we learn to get in touch with our feelings can we commence the (highly-fulfilling and often mind-altering) process of breaking through this superficial veneer we've created and start connecting with our authentic self. From that point on, connecting and sharing with others, letting them know the real you, is bound to become a whole lot easier, perhaps even something to look forward to.

Checking Out Our Story

We each have individual stories, reasons, even traumas underpinning our CF behaviours. Knowing what our story is, digging around in our history to locate key causal factors, helps build the awareness crucial for self-development. No need to sink into blame games or victim mode ("My parents did this to me – they completely f*cked me up"; "I'd be successful by now if that hadn't happened") – that only takes us away from the task at hand. The point is to get in touch with why these controlling behaviours manifested for us in the first place. And that whole process starts by looking inwards and checking out what's there.

Now is as good a time as any to start thinking about what your story might be. Here are several ideas to help you tap into your inner world:

1. Find a relaxing environment and sit or lay down. Either close your eyes or keep your eyes open and focus on a stable object – pick something boring and inanimate (not your favourite TV show or the hottie sunbathing next door). Resist the temptation to *do* anything. Just be with your mind and body. Thoughts will flood your mind like "What a waste of time", or "God, I'm soooo bored right now", or even "I'll be making some sweet loving tonight (accompanied by uncensored visual images)". While it's near impossible to resist them – don't even bother trying the resistance tactic, it usually makes those thoughts multiply – thoughts like these are to be expected. They pop up because the mind doesn't want you to stop for a breather and just be quiet in a space of observation. It's too busy grasping onto whatever images and thoughts come along, letting fears run amok, and keeping dramas alive and well. That's okay, that's just the nature of an out-of-control mind; simply observe any thoughts you notice come up. See if you can detach yourself from the thoughts, stepping away from them in a sense, watching

them as you'd watch a cloud pass by. Pay attention to how your mind chases after thoughts, aching to grasp onto one so it can sink into a thinking cycle. Taking time to observe your mind, becoming intimately familiar with how it operates, is by far the most rewarding activity you can do as far as cultivating self-awareness is concerned.

2. Start a diary or journal, if you don't have one already. Try a blank (un-ruled) notebook – I find they're the best as you can be as creatively wild as you want, way beyond the restrictions of a ruled line format. Once you've grabbed your journal and a pen, before you start writing, sit still and notice what's there for you – any emotions activated or feelings making their way to the surface? By settling down a restless monkey mind at the outset, you'll have much more success when listening in to what's going on beneath. Once you've reached a level of stillness, write with the aim of bypassing logic and reason, getting into all the intuitive, feeling stuff that lies beneath ("How I feel about my Father passing away is…..."; "All this conflict at work makes me feel…..."; "When I think about being job-less for so long, it feels….."). Try limiting your writing to *you* – don't go on about how other people are messing up your life – it's completely irrelevant here. Stick to what's happening with you and in you – everything else, all the stuff going on in the external world, is beside the point and needs to be dropped. Taking this exercise on with the fervour of Plato is guaranteed to get you more than a few gold insights!

3. For a twist on journal writing, switch to writing with your non-dominant hand. "How ludicrous!" I hear CFs everywhere declare in almost deafening tones. Not really. This technique helps you access the right side of your brain responsible for creativity and feeling. Sidestepping all the logic, it gets straight to the heart of the matter, often revealing a raft of subconscious thoughts, feelings and memories. For an added surprise, try writing from a totally different perspective – as if you were eight years old (replace with two, four, or twelve – anything is fine here). Drop any hint of perfectionism, of feeling more than a bit weird, and don't even try to write half as well as your dominant hand – too much of an effort. Just go with the flow and enjoy the controlled loss of control. You may well be amazed at what comes out!

4. If you're connected to your artistic spirit (it's even better if you're not), grab a few crayons (yes, those kiddie play things) and pieces of paper, and draw what you're feeling. Try not to think too much about this – the point is to express your feelings. The best time to do this is after you've spent some quiet time contemplating your controlling behaviours. Allow your inner child room for expression and – here is the fun part – don't resist it! Play away!!

Perhaps with some apprehension, we might curiously seek out both our light and dark parts – that is, what we perceive to be the 'good' and 'bad' bits of our personality. Our CF self is comprised of a number of techniques and behaviours we've developed to deal with those things we typically feel unable to cope with. In those moments of getting in touch with the emotions and feelings behind the behaviour, we start seeing ourselves for *all* of who we are, not merely the good bits we generally like to focus on and project into the world. A new world of awareness is given space to emerge and we begin noticing the things that trigger us into feeling the need to control. Perhaps even more importantly, we learn to recognise how this makes us feel in our emotional and physical bodies. That's what 'getting out of your head' is all about – an opportunity to get to know all of you, not just the mind chatter you typically relate to as you.

There is no greater light than the incandescent glow of self-awareness to guide us through darkness to the manifestation of our unique true self. Sound corny? Put another way... navel gazing can heighten our self-knowledge exponentially, clearing though the age-old fears that have held us back, and helping us relax into our authentic self. Taking time to genuinely reflect back on our lives and our stories is truly rewarding. Not only that, but our mind receives a clear signal that our needs and self-growth are worthy of our attention. Many people think CFs value themselves over everyone and everything else, but that's not always the case. Committing to self-enquiry confirms you're a really important person in your world. It says "Bring it on" – showing readiness and courage to do the challenging inner work most people won't.

TEN

MANAGING LIFE'S UNCERTAINTY

For those of you who flicked directly to this page, ignoring all the info in previous chapters deeming it 'non-essential', would you please just exercise a modicum of patience, go back to Chapter One, and start from there? You can't expect to jump on a fast-track to awareness and insightful self-growth; it just doesn't work that way. This isn't a 'Get Wise Quick' scheme. You have got to put in the hard yards, consistently doing the work it takes to develop a deep understanding about how you work – your fundamental mental/emotional mechanics.

For those who diligently read through the previous chapters, maybe having had a bit of a chuckle completing the questionnaire, perhaps even picking up an idea or insight here and there, I can almost hear you say "Finally, a practical solution... just give it to me now", in true CF style. When it comes to getting the info they need, CFs love cutting to the chase, getting to the crux of the subject. Their 'knowing' something is of paramount importance when it comes to being able to foresee how things could play out – similar to an early warning system. Yet this intolerance for 'extraneous' detail can often come back and bite them if a detrimental dose of impatience leads them to cut corners and miss key pieces of the message. So, let's jump on in to the how-to of managing life's uncertainty…

Let's start here: you don't really think you can manage uncertainty, do you? Seriously? Well, if you're a CF, you probably do. After all, that's the primary objective of all CF thinking and behaviours. CFs have this loose wiring going on where they truly believe they're able to manage life in such a way that uncertainty gets to play the most insignificant of roles. On the one hand, it's so nice to live in that delusion; you've got your own little megalomaniac kingdom where you are the ruler of your world. On the other hand… well, you're just conning yourself into believing something that simply isn't true. As a (mostly) reformed CF, I thought exactly the same way until I dared to pull the veil off my (rather disillusioned) way of perceiving the world. Now, let's drop the illusion and take a look at how life really is...

Managing Others as a Form of Control

Management is an esteemed (or despised) word in this day and age, as are the people who practice it – managers. The core function of management is to take charge in order to ensure a desirable outcome – a CF's dream role! Managers are there to seize control, using weapons as fierce as verbal directives and statistical pie charts to steer the organisation/

team in the direction it needs to go. In managerial mode, we're attempting to assert a degree of control or structure around business activities and the people tasked to complete them (i.e. our loyal subjects). Managers take on huge responsibility for achieving outcomes from their team, based on objectives defined within a broader business strategy/plan. Before shouldering any responsibility, they require an assurance of two things – control around their teams output, and the required resources needed to get the job done (e.g. adequate number of capable staff and funding).

To be at all effective, management has at its foundation a rigorous approach to shaping the way people deliver the necessary outcomes. The manager defines and monitors (read: analyse, assess, analyse again) exactly what's required to get from A to Z. When an individual or team prove their competency in delivering on agreed outcomes, the manager usually starts to develop trust (unless they're an extreme CF, who finds it near to impossible to trust anyone), and loosens the degree of control, including any bothersome micromanagement checks initially set in place. Plans have been followed, controls acknowledged, targets reached – a degree of certainty has crept in based on a proven track record. Yet the management leash is swiftly tightened if the results start to drop off, or if there's any other indication of the individual or team having adopted a wayward approach to their work. Typical carrot and stick tactics – carrot if you're good, whack with a stick if you're bad.

In my career as an Organisational Change Manager and Professional Coach, I've come across only a few managers who steer a team or project with a minimum degree of structure or control in place. The ones I have met usually struggle with team effectiveness – their staff end up running their own show, and any chance of delivering the necessary outcomes within a specified budget or timeframe becomes quite an ordeal. So it seems clearly evident that CFs are a natural fit for the command-and-control style management approach still so prevalent in business today – "You want me to control a group of people to achieve whatever results I deem appropriate, however I see fit to do so? Sounds right up my alley!" They take to it like a duck to water. Competent management requires an ability to plan and control things and people – the thing CFs do really, really well. The downside here is that management roles can exaggerate a CF's controlling tendencies by reinforcing those behaviours through reward and recognition of a job well done. This behavioural reinforcement, gained predominantly in business life, can make it enormously tough for CFs to let go of and give up this way of being that so often cripples them in their personal lives.

When we experience success through rolling out our controlling behaviours at work, we often draw a link – controlling and structuring one part of our life could be transferable to other parts too. The project plan that delivered our business initiative could also be used to bring structure to the seemingly random nature of the family home. Wow! Or the strategies and rewards used to guide employees towards higher productivity could also be used to steer teenagers or partners towards our desired outcomes. Wow!!!!! Thinking we've found a magic formula bound to fix-up and streamline every troublesome element in our lives, we naively apply these tactics and managerial competencies to our personal lives, expecting to achieve the same level of success. But, more often than we care to admit, things backfire. We find ourselves relating to our partners/kids/friends the same way we relate to an employee who's refused to follow our instructions. We think and act like we're in charge – and we really want to be – but clearly we're not. We're still trying to manage everything 'out there' without even considering how much more effective it would be to manage stuff 'in here'.

Greg realised the usual carrot and stick approach
might not work with Rodney.

Self-Management as a Form of Control

Then there's the (almost) opposite end of the spectrum - those uptight CFs who feel the need to control themselves as well as everything external to them. These individuals usually believe they're absolute geniuses when it comes to self-management. They walk around with pursed or tightly-locked lips, a mind so closed it's hard to prise it open to any new idea, and a body so stiff you could iron a shirt on it. Schedules, to-do lists, goal setting, and time management are all part of this CF's existence. Their motto – life needs structure and I'm here to give it that! Self-help books, popular magazines, TV shows, coaches, and personal development gurus all encourage us to create structures that support us in life. Most of the time this information is hugely supportive – helping us to lose weight, get healthy, take responsibility, plan and reach goals, and rejuvenate struggling relationships. But to a CF, these suggestions can be applied with so much rigour and inflexibility that they result in organising life to such a severe degree there's little to no room to move. The lack of adaptability that comes with rigid routines creates a mechanical robot-style approach to life, where things must be a certain way before all the good stuff's allowed to occur.

When we're so uptight that we feel the need to control everything we do, say and feel, our behaviours fall at the extreme end of the CF spectrum. Dictatorial self-management further reinforces our inner CF, constantly pushing ourselves to the limit to achieve what we think we need, in ways we honestly believe are serving us. Even minor 'wins' can support the belief that controlling and disciplining ourselves left, right and centre is the way to go. It's the masochist's path to self-success – whipping yourself into compliance. A strict and demanding form of self-management keeps us boxed into habitual patterns and screams mistrust of self. Being utterly anxious about what would happen if we were to relax and let go, we end up denying ourselves the very thing we're seeking – to live a happy and fulfilling life.

A Healthy Kind of Control

Let me clarify an important point here. Not *all* controlling behaviours are dysfunctional. Typically, the kinds of behaviours that have had us branded a CF are the types which are directed externally – when we're trying to control someone or something in our environment. On the flip side, a healthy balance of self-control (as opposed to the authoritarian type) is imperative for attaining personal goals, increasing confidence and self-worth. People have more of a severe reaction when someone's trying to control them than when they're noticing the effects of someone demonstrating self-control, which is often a lot less perceptible and certainly more acceptable.

A balanced proportion of self-control is a good look – it indicates a willingness to take responsibility for our life. Instead of expecting our external world to fulfil our needs and meet our demands, we rely on internal resources to manage and satisfy our everyday requirements. That includes acknowledging our wants may not always be fulfilled on a daily basis and being able to accept that reality without throwing a tantrum. This equates to being willing, if not always able, to manage our reactions and responses to whatever we encounter in our lives. Importantly, it also translates to having less of a need for situations and people to be a certain way in order for us to stay centred and relaxed – we become a lot less reactive and much more responsive to the situation at hand. Unfortunately, in a world where self-gratification and addiction to the pleasure principle at almost any cost has risen to unparalleled levels, self-control seems more and more to be a heavily under-utilised capability. The concept and practice of delayed gratification, a key indicator of success and life fulfilment, seems to have slipped into irrelevance as the give-it-to-me-now era makes its mark on the world.

Self-management is immensely useful as a means to help CFs develop a gentle and supportive structure for life, and work through issues of self-trust and discipline. It can even be utilised to schedule in the time and space required for some full-on self-enquiry and self-care. Where it comes unstuck and renders itself useless, even destructive, is when our focus remains external and we don't bother doing the hard yards to turn responsibility and the focal point back to ourselves. Positive change will only ever come when we turn our focus inwards and completely resist the urge to manage and control the world around us.

Cultivating a healthy self-control works magic for us in these key ways:

➤ It places the focus firmly back where it needs to be – on ourselves;

➤ It sets firm yet supportive boundaries for us to develop ourselves within;

➤ It helps us build self-esteem and self-worth;

➤ It supports us in feeling confident enough to let go of the control reins;

➤ It enables us to start building trust in ourselves that we can deal with challenges;

➤ It assists us in structuring our lives in ways that aid goal achievement;

➤ It builds clarity around our priorities and activities;

➤ It enhances our ability to deal with the uncertainty and ambiguity in life.

Lots of highly beneficial stuff!

The Only Constant is Change

It was Heraclitus the Greek philosopher who said "Everything flows, nothing stands still" and "Nothing endures but change". Wise words indeed; as relevant today as they've ever been. We simply can't dispute the fact that life's in a constant state of flux. Just look around – things are being born, decaying and dying all over the place – nothing ever really stands still. Because of the ceaseless nature of change, the impermanent character of life, uncertainty has to be recognised as an indirect consequence. With all the change taking place around us, we can't ever expect to know 100% how things will evolve over time. Yet so many of us (and pretty much all CFs) cling to what can only be described as a deluded perception that people (personalities, preferences, beliefs, values, opinions) and circumstances are somehow set in stone, and we have minimal tolerance for any variances to this. We're pulling the wool over our eyes when such rigid thinking stops us seeing possible alternatives – talk about setting ourselves up for disappointment!

By looking at life with even a fraction of objectivity, we can see how change permeates everything – fluctuation and impermanence are everywhere. A far cry from those high-speed documentaries that capture a year's worth of movement in a two-minute snapshot, change on a day-to-day basis isn't always that noticeable. But it's always there. Like growing taller in adolescence (and shorter in old age), the increments can be miniscule and only recognisable when measured every once in a while. Then there's the type of change that doesn't have any noticeable physical manifestation. Like the shifts we have mentally, emotionally or energetically – we feel the change inside, but the effects aren't necessarily noticed directly or immediately, particularly by others. Changes that are most obvious are the ones accompanied by bigger shifts, towards the 'positive' or 'negative'. What's 'positive' for one person can be significantly 'negative' for another – a variation on the 'glass half full' concept. Whatever subjective perceptions we thrust on the change around us, one thing's certain – the massive complexity of life shows change is a constant occurrence, and we can never sanely expect to be fully in control.

By acknowledging change as an inescapable facet of everyday life, we can tolerate, accept or embrace the changes that do occur. Denial, frustration, even tolerance, suggests resistance to what is. Tolerance is when you put up with something – a far cry from a state of acceptance. There's no flow in any form of resistance, just an uncomfortable, rocky ride. We love to think we can control most of the outcomes in our life, but the simple truth is we can't ever do that completely. Strangely enough, other people have their own ideas as to where they want to go and what they want to do, and this doesn't necessarily always align with what we're hoping to attain. When we resist what is (the way the world works, people's choices, any curve balls thrown our way, the outcomes that are showing up), we're stuck in our own little world of delusion.

When we truly begin accepting that change is an inherent characteristic of life, in its own impervious way, an allowance starts to take shape. No longer is there an anxiety-ridden need to control external outcomes; the focus on influencing outcomes turns inward. The best chance I have of shaping and accepting the outcomes in my world is through adjusting my perspective and bringing my best characteristics to the table. The energy and effort once spent trying to make the world adapt to our needs and desires is now dedicated to helping ourselves grow, so that we can feel capable of dealing with any situation that comes our way. The greatest life-altering changes occur within; the most profound contribution we can make is in the changed self we bring to the world.

"You must be the change you want to see in the world."

Mahatma Gandhi

Keeping Us on Our Toes

How often do we hear of someone having gone through a tumultuous event only to have come out of it with a different understanding, attitude or approach to life? We need challenges in life to learn; the hardship and uncertainty we face helps us grow and mature. The unpredictable, while at times downright unpleasant, can serve us enormously as a tool for building our resilience muscles and testing our composure. Uncertainty keeps us on our toes, encouraging a flexible attitude over an anxious and uptight one. The reality of not knowing serves to remind us of the immense possibilities that letting go of the need to know can bring to our daily existence.

As CFs, we struggle to no end with accepting the possibilities associated with uncertainty, simply because we doubt our own ability to deal effectively with unexpected change. Even though experience proved to me I always landed on my feet through challenging times of change, I still never believed in myself enough to trust I could handle any situation that came my way. Ignoring all the background evidence that I could cope, it was like having a default mechanism clicking in – change generates fear, which gives rise to anxiety, activating my insecurities, which inevitably leads to me thinking "F*ck! I can't deal with this!!" Massive apprehension towards change manifested rather speedily through continuous rumination and worry about how things could end up going disastrously pear-shaped. All the proof of my capacity over the years to deal with life's ordeals was paid not an ounce of attention, clouded over then blocked out by increasing levels of anxiety. At this stage, I had a way to go before I learned that life is able and eager to support me, if only I trust it to do so.

Since those dark days of disillusionment, I've come to acknowledge that challenges presented to me in life can be seen as either troublesome burdens or valuable gifts (even if it's tough to first see their value). Seeing now how the curve balls that come my way are the Universe's way of saying "Okay, let's see what you've learned", I know the right mind-set and belief in my abilities will demonstrate that I'm more than capable of coming out the other side, and a bit wiser for having undergone the challenge. In my heart and head, the shift from a fundamental mistrust in everything to one of having trust and faith that I can indeed get through the tough times, has not only helped me become more well-balanced, it's made me a hell of a lot easier to be around.

Screwed Up by Expectations

When we're expecting something to occur, we place lots of hope and energy into the possibility of it happening. We might visualise getting that promotion we've been chasing for the last two years, have wildly erotic fantasies about our gorgeous new work colleague, or daydream about the fun we're going to have on next month's adventure holiday to Mongolia. All the images and scripts we play out in our minds project our desires onto some future event we hope will transpire exactly as we've imagined it. In our little fantasy land, we picture/hear certain scenarios playing out, and any associated emotions build as we anticipate the outcome over and over again.

Then when the actual event rolls around, something different happens – not at all like the fantasy land vision we imagined. The more emotions invested in our (completely-devoid-of-reality) daydreaming, the more difficult it is to accept what actually happens. "I mean, come on, it should have worked out the way I wanted it to. Right?" Wrong! Unless we're stuck in a repetitive déjà vu scene, like Bill Murray's character in 'Groundhog Day', we can't ever hope to accurately forecast what's going to happen in any given scenario. Especially when it involves other people and places we're unfamiliar with – this really escalates the unpredictability factor. The more variables, the more chances that a very different outcome than the one we've anticipated will occur. When things don't work out the way we hoped, it inevitably leads to feelings of disappointment, sadness, bitterness, anger, even fear. Our expectations are the root cause of the majority of the upsets we have in life, primarily because we do such a damned good job of buying into those picture-perfect fantasy scenarios we've dreamt about and want so much.

CFs generally believe the outcomes we're aiming for will surely come to be if only we try hard enough (i.e. exert enough control over everything) to make sure it happens. It's a grand delusion built to cover up fears of a fundamentally unsafe world. And if it doesn't turn out the way we want it to, well, we assume we just need to exert more effort (read: control) next time to make sure things do turn out the way they're meant to. In this respect, as CFs we have more invested in our expectations than most other people – the outcomes that do show up for us reflect just how successful we've been in our ability to control all and sundry. This, in turn, taps into and builds confidence in being able to manage uncertainty and insecurity within, keeping our anxiety demons at bay.

Living a life jam-packed with expectations primarily means one thing – living somewhere other than the present. When expectations play a major role in our lives, we're either off frolicking about in the future, dreaming up what could be, or stepping back into the past, either licking our wounds or blowing our trumpets over how things turned out. Think of it as a form of escapism. Our current situational state is so uncomfortable, so unbearable, that we prefer being elsewhere. And that elsewhere is milling around in fantasy land in our minds. Now, you might believe you don't think of your present situation as intolerable. And my question to you is "Well then, why do you spend so much time running away from it by constantly thinking about what has happened or what could be?" Reality can't be found anywhere but here and now. And yet, for the vast majority of people, both CFs and non-CFs, it's a reality we're continually trying to avoid by using a multitude of escapist tactics. Why? Because being in the here and now requires that we are okay with ourselves, willing to confront our fears head-on, comfortable with the inherent uncertainty in life, and feeling confidently capable of handling any given situation. Most of us find that pretty hard to achieve.

We could all use a lesson or two in letting go of expectations!

Our (Often Vain and Amusing) Attempts at Managing Uncertainty

By far the most powerful influence we have on life is the command over our own beliefs, attitudes and behaviours. Exerting most of our influence and control externally in attempts to manage uncertainty and fulfil daydream expectations not only leads to a whole lot of frustration, it also has an enormous impact on our mental and emotional energy levels. At one time or another, every CF is bound to have noticed how tiring it is being the master strategist of our personal universe. Worrying, analysing, planning, concocting – all these thoughts and tactical responses churn through an incredible amount of mind activity. Some of us are so good at planning, plotting and strategizing, we can't consciously catch ourselves in the act of doing it. It's like being on auto-pilot; we never dare query the reasons behind our taking certain steps or why something is the way it is. Instead, we notice the effects – feeling tired, drained, lethargic, angry, and irritable – but don't always link that back to the causal factor: our crazy controlling behaviours seeking ultimate domination so we don't have to feel so scared. When we think about all the effort we put into adjusting and manipulating certain situations and people, we start seeing how much time and energy we invest in these pursuits. It can be bloody exhausting! Time and energy that's better spent paying attention to sorting ourselves out on the inside, helping us become more able to respond to unexpected outcomes with maturity and wisdom, instead of anxiety and paranoia.

As CFs, we strive to create a perfect future, devoid of far-too-hard ordeals and nasty surprises, and do so with a fervent belief that the future can be controlled according to our precise requirements. On varying levels, CFs don't want to accept that the Universe/God/Nature works in mysterious ways. Even the most ardent CF religious believers, self-declared persons of faith, adamantly refuse to go with the flow, and just don't get that life isn't meant to be predictable. Imagine what it would be like if, shortly after birth, we were provided with a full life itinerary – at seven years of age you'll break your leg in a bike accident... your forty-fourth year will see you get married for a third time... you'll cease to exist at age sixty-eight due a rogue elephant stampede while on safari in Botswana – not much choice or freedom in that option. How about an alternative – being blessed with the power to plan exactly what we want upfront and have all of it delivered exactly as we wish. I'm not sure that would work unless our authority extends to include everyone's universe. There goes any chance of changing our minds. And freedom of choice for everyone else gets thrown out the window too – way too 'me' focused and narcissistic.

"As I said, our life forecasts are 100% accurate.
When it says that little Chloe will run away and join
the circus at 13, you can rest assured it's correct."

As the need for surety and control escalates, the CF's modus operandi is revealed and includes a wide range of tactics aimed at preventing the undesirable. Here's a taste of some of the more popular and distasteful ones:

- Ignore, silence or dismiss the opinions of others, and use reason to support ours;
- Withdraw attention or affection to make someone behave the way we want them to;
- Raise our voice or shout in an argument to make a person back down or give up;
- Instruct others on how they should act, think and be – in case they're getting it all wrong;
- Use manipulative tactics designed to persuade others to our point of view.

No matter how shrewd and/or bullying our tactics get, efforts to swing the game our way don't always work – thank goodness! However structured, manipulative, or controlling we are, attempts at harnessing destiny don't always result in what we planned for. More often than not, the harder we try – the added frustration, expectation and anxiety we pour into our efforts – the more egg we get on our faces if it doesn't work. We expend so much effort directing everything and everyone else, we completely forget to address the core element that ultimately defines our life – our individual state of mind. Not anyone or anything out there, external to us, is going to shape what outcomes show up in our lives more than we will. The focus just has to turn inward if we're to have any chance at all of living a life free of anxiety, frustration and insecurity.

Once we start dealing with all the screwed up perceptions and beliefs we have relating to ourselves and life in general, we're in a much better position to contribute to outcomes going our way. Taking on a balanced approach to self-management, we're more likely to start assuming responsibility for our attitudes and behaviours, not using others in attempts to fend off our fears and insecurities. Keeping the focus within, we're able to exert greater influence over these other bits and pieces in life:

- The people in our life (those that still choose to stay around);
- Events (where we go, when we go, what we see/do);
- Plans (personal/family goals and associated timelines);
- Environment (where we live/work/eat/drink);
- Health (staying fit, eating right, having regular check-ups).

No matter how first-rate our self-management is, at times life gets in the way and has a cheeky way of reminding us that, in real terms, we're not always in the driver's seat. Even when it's clear we have no say in or influence over a situation, we still have control over the most important part – how we respond or react to what goes on. If our self-management includes a healthy dose of support, nurturing and self-reflection, we're going to be way better off in terms of being able to deal with whatever life throws at us. And if things which you have little or no control over go awfully wrong, like this...

- Your partner has an affair and/or leaves you;
- You're diagnosed with a life-threatening illness;
- A car goes through a red light and crashes into your car and you're in it – ouch!!
- Your position at the company you've been with for 15 years is made redundant;
- A loved one dies.

… you'll be able to bring a higher degree of awareness to the situation which will, hopefully, help you through such challenges.

Alternatives to Managing Uncertainty

Just as the only constant in life is change, the only thing really certain in life is uncertainty. We can struggle against uncertainty and reality all we want, but ultimately it does no one any good. With all the energy, effort, frustration and anxiety associated with controlling behaviours, one has to wonder at some point if attempting to manage the uncertainty of life is the best approach. Self-management is one thing – we can be reasonably assured of getting our intended results if we put enough discipline, diligence and patience into it –

but all the trouble we put into managing external elements, which often have a random mind of their own, just doesn't seem to be worth it. It makes a lot more sense to take all that (often wasted) energy we exert meddling with the hard-to-control externals, and instead apply it internally to developing an acceptance of uncertainty and a keener awareness of our own perspectives and behaviours. By acknowledging that we will never be able to control life's uncertainty, we can then let go of our need to manage everything and start relaxing into life.

Perhaps then we could change the title of this section from 'Managing Life's Uncertainty' to...

Accepting Life's Uncertainty

Ah, that's better! For some CFs, the idea of accepting uncertainty rather than managing it can seem to be a bit of a cop out – surrendering your power to the otherwise inevitable. There's a part deep inside every CF that would scream "NNOOOOOO!!!" to the idea, grasping onto every last thread of control as the anxiety demons rear their ugly heads. Once we recognise that change is inevitable and could even be in our best interests, we seriously need to start finding ways to get comfortable with life's grey ambiguity. We'll never be motivated to let go of the control strings if we can't accept this inherent quality of uncertainty in life and start trusting that we'll be able to deal with the highs and lows as we ride through it.

When we adopt an accepting attitude, we move from managing mode (implying a nosey need for control) to a 'go with the flow' perspective (suggesting an acknowledgement that certain details are simply outside our control) – undoubtedly the biggest shift a CF needs to make. This signals a letting go; a trust that life will work out in ways that support and grow us – the key factor in transitioning to new beliefs and behaviours. Accepting is closely related to surrendering – you surrender to the possibility and you accept whatever outcomes come to pass. Note: acceptance doesn't necessarily mean you have to agree with an outcome; but struggling with an outcome is pretty much useless – you're best off accepting it in the present and proactively taking action to change it going forward.

Of course, fears will unavoidably rise up, encouraging us against taking this path. Moving towards acceptance provides an ideal opportunity to dig down deep into our fears, getting to the bottom and finally knowing the answer to the mostly-avoided question: "What am I afraid of?" Over time, control has masked the fears, so when we decide to step away from our stereotypical behaviours, we end up staring our fears in the face – an extremely uncomfortable confrontation. Especially if we're arrogant and ignorant enough to believe we're pretty much fearless and could take on the world and win – hugely deflating for an ego of that magnitude. Being presented with our fears is like staring down the biggest, scariest demons – you just ache to run in the opposite direction and hide under a bed somewhere. But remember this is tough work that will rid us of fear-based thinking and allow us to unleash our authentic selves – and we're tough enough to take it on! Yeah!! Note: At this point, if beating your chest or punching the air in front of you makes you feel a whole lot tougher or more inspired, go ahead, knock yourself out!

Wait…it doesn't end there. There's another huge step after acceptance which catapults us into an entirely new way of being in and relating to the world. Let's leap into...

Embracing Life's Uncertainty

Wow, even scarier (I mean 'better')!! A huge change takes place between being fearful of anything we can't predict and really embracing change with a bring-it-on attitude. The difference between accepting and embracing uncertainty is in seeing uncertainty as an opportunity – to learn, to stretch, to change, to grow. As a 'yet-to-start-the-self-development-path' CF, we perceive uncertainty as inherently dangerous or, at best, vaguely tolerable. As a CF who's transitioned to the acceptance stage, there's a lot more comfort in working with what we've got to play with, happily dropping any resistance attitudes, and being okay with what is. When we move into embracing change, it's like a paradigm shift – we view it through a lens of possibility: "I wonder how this will play out; it could radically alter my knowledge, my being, my life for the better." It's all about seeing beyond what may initially be tagged as a dilemma or problem, staying receptive to whatever doors open up, even if there's a mega-dose of sadness, grief or pain delivered by the ones closing.

Getting to this stage is a long, hard road for CFs. The old tagline "It won't happen overnight, but it will happen" is right on the mark here. Most people, regardless of whether they're CFs or not, experience massive resistance to accepting, let alone embracing, all of life's surprise offerings, struggling continually with what is. I'll occasionally have an internal wrestling match when it comes to welcoming unsettling circumstances into my life, having to stop myself from slipping too deeply into feelings of unease and anxiety, with an ache for control rising in the background. Embracing uncertainty requires us to have stared down our biggest fears, and found some reason for and relief from the pain underneath. Demanding complete trust in our ability to handle any Pandora's Box opened before us, it provides a golden opportunity to see whatever we're served with as a chance for humungous self-growth. Here we enter the field of potentiality, playing in the space of possibility and co-creativity, a state of remaining totally open to whatever manifests (the area of Quantum Mechanics made popular by the 'What the Bleep Do We Know' doco). A miniscule number of people live consistently in this state, and I'm certainly not one of them – many CFs and non-CFs alike find the work and patience required to get there far too difficult. But it is achievable…

Living in the present, being more accepting of our life situation, is a big ask of ourselves, but the benefits are enormous.

Just imagine what it would be like not having to bust your gut to ensure everything is exactly as you think it should be. To not have to spend loads of your precious time and energy worrying about how things are going to turn out. Not having the need to constantly defend yourself against all the potentially horrible outcomes you've envisaged in your nightmare fantasy land. In fact, to not even ever think of horrible events that may or may not come to be. To feel confident and courageous enough to know you'll be able to deal with anything that's dished onto your plate; feeling completely at ease and at peace with whatever comes about.

Imagine that... pretty cool, huh?

ELEVEN

LIVING WHAT IS

Having discovered that attempts at managing uncertainty are way more likely to reinforce the CF mindset than placate it, let's now continue our exploration, inquiring into the oft uninhabitable world of living what is. I say "oft uninhabitable" for good reason. Let's face it – relatively few of us live in a state of harmony with the life process. Our days are often peppered with gripes, bitching and struggling to accept reality. Those that seem to have managed to somehow 'get their shit together' are usually revered and quickly stamped with a guru label ("Her meditative state is so sublime, I feel like I'm meditating too just being in her presence" or "He rocks when it comes to living out his potential; the guy's a legend"). Whether we're up for being tagged a guru or not, let's take a look at how we can let go of the CF stranglehold and start stepping into the flow...

Jumping Off the CF Treadmill

Feeling in control of situations and people around us can have almost intoxicating effects. Not everyone gets a high from being the self-declared playwright, producer and director of their life circumstances, but for CFs it borders on euphoric, particularly when everything goes to plan. In these circumstances, it's easy to convince ourselves we really are the master of our Universe – a belief which morphs into a high and mighty attitude verging on God mentality. To intentionally want to let go of this power trip seems completely insane from a highly-charged CF perspective. Why would you ever seriously even think of forfeiting power and control in a world that lives and breathes it? Crazy stuff!

When we spend a huge chunk of life controlling people and things left, right and centre, at some point (if we're a tad switched on) we come to realise that being a CF isn't all it's cut out to be. It's exhausting running the show all the time, stressing out if the slightest thing goes wrong. Although uncomfortably comfortable in their way of being, some CFs may be considering whether it's time to tread the (rather intimidating) path of self-transformation. The thought of living in a way that releases our tight, controlling grasp on life scares the hell out of most CFs, going against everything we understand to be sensible and safe. Stuck in controlling and habitual patterns, addicted to the relief it provides for our anxious minds, we struggle to truly connect with the downsides of our behaviour, focusing only on the rather superficial benefits we do receive.

When things are planned to a more-or-less predictable level (excepting the odd surprise here and there), there certainly is less to fear. Except one thing – BOREDOM! CFs typically have a chronic lack of spontaneity in their lives, living within the confines of tightly controlled parameters ("This must happen in order for this to occur, which will result in the perfect outcome"). When everything is known or predictable, the fun, the spice of life, is perilously extracted. For the majority of CFs, it's a trade-off they choose to live with mostly because they don't know what they're missing and are just too frightened of letting go of the control reins. Living predictably, in our nicely defined comfort zone, may have its rewards – there's more of a sense of certainty in terms of what it is we want to have and accomplish, and how we go about getting there – but it will never give us the 100% safety guarantee we hope for. Nor will it allow us to grow into 'together' individuals who embody self-trust and self-responsibility and are more than keen to savour the many and varied flavours life has to offer.

Once a CF decides to step off the control treadmill, anxiety inevitably appears. It's not if, it's how and when. Similar to addictive behaviour, when we start self-regulation around habitual CF behaviours, we're going to strike a chord or two. On hearing the "DANGER, DANGER" warning bells going off in response to a threat on the psyche's status quo, our change resistor kicks in to assess what's going on and re-establish some sense of equilibrium. Keep in mind that controlling behaviours are in place to help us deal with everyday anxiety, and any attempts to remove safeguards will attract major resistance. When we hit the override button and our key protective behaviours are bypassed, we open the gate to a barrage of anxieties we've attempted to keep at bay. Like a detox, all the muck unavoidably rises to the surface, which can be a hugely unsettling experience to say the least. But there are ways to prepare for this onslaught of discomfort and manage our resistance demons. Check out Chapter Twelve for a few tips on managing the muck.

Liberating Your Inner Rebel

As a CF, I reached a point where I realised that if I wanted to live a full and meaningful life, I had to start challenging my perceptions – about myself, my life, and what was on offer. Up until then, I'd seen life as something you mostly struggled through. Sure, there were ups as well as downs, but for me, the ups took a lot to reach. And when I did get a win, it was often clouded with doubt and anxiousness, and I found myself struggling to revel in post-achievement glory. Whenever a pinnacle was reached, I began worrying about how I could stay there, if I deserved to be there, and what potential dangers were lurking around the corner waiting to bump me off my little podium. On top of all the anxiety-ridden thinking, I started looking for the next pinnacle to reach, never fully satisfied with a win or the hard yards it had taken to get there. So bloody exhausting and lacking in fulfilment!

Due to circumstances wholly within my control, at the not-so-tender age of forty-one I created an opportunity to free myself more than momentarily from the monotonous world of business; to escape for an undefined amount of time into the adventurous world of solo international travel. Call it a premature mid-life crisis or not, I was bucking up against the status quo at a time in life when everyone knew (and made sure to remind me) that one's primary focus should be on building financial security and consolidating career achievements. Nearly a year of travelling forced me to let go of the rigidity I'd imposed on my life and get some spontaneity happening. Faced with new environments, languages and cultures (from China to the U.K to Egypt to Scandinavia to Israel to most of Europe), I felt way out of control. I was out of control with no idea what might come my way at any time. It felt like swirling around in a void with nothing to cling on to. In the early days there were moments of almost sheer terror at what I was doing (a particular time being when the bird flu epidemic hit the news in the middle of my travels through rural China). But I persisted despite the fears and had the time of my life (to date).

I turned into a bit of a rebel in my early forties, verging on the proverbial bohemian (well almost), and I've never looked back. Questioning society's status quo – the one we're all encouraged to buy into, and usually do – I wondered if there could be a different way of living life. I queried my own worldview too, taking a reality check on my beliefs around how I thought things should be, and realised life whizzes by far too quickly to play it safe all the time. So many people stay stuck in their beliefs and life routines, scared to step outside their carefully contrived box, tolerating a dull existence simply because it's what they are used to. They miss out on a plethora of opportunities and adventures, their fears keeping them trapped inside lives which may feel meaningless to them. There can be immense beauty in letting go and trusting that life will guide you to where you need to be. It's just a matter of connecting with your inner rebel and gathering the guts to confront your fears.

Here are a few ways to connect into your rebel self (outside of getting a Harley or a tattoo):

➢ Write a list of what you're settling for in life – things that provide no joy or meaning and are there simply because you're afraid of letting go and stepping into an alternative.

➢ Remember what lights your fire? Or has it been so long since you've connected to it that it's merely a distant memory? Work at tapping into that fire once more and jot down some ideas on what ignites those sparks. Never been lit up? Dig into memories or access those dreams you've kept hidden away somewhere in your psyche. Then look at how you might start releasing and expressing those.

➢ Think of something you want to do, but have been more than a bit timid about doing it. Write it down. Note a few points on why you haven't carried it out, as well as the points 'for' and 'against' doing it. Then visualise two future possibilities – one continuing on the path you're already on (no changes or an exacerbation of what's already showing up); the other having undertaken the action and changed direction. Write down what comes up for you (thoughts, visions, fears) and reflect on whether potential changes can be committed to.

Living in Presence

"All the while it is the present only."

Walt Whitman

For the vast majority of us, the idea of living fully in the present is more than a bit odd. I mean, isn't a present what you give someone as a gift? How do you live in that? Well, yes, but the present I'm referring to here is a point in time – one that's always ticking over. The present moment is fleeting, but it's the only place we can fully experience the reality of what is. We can ponder over our future, attempting to predict or manipulate upcoming events, but this is a made-up idea of how things will be – more hope and/or delusion than reality. Or we can delve into our pasts, rehashing old conversations and outcomes, savouring good memories and editing others as we see fit. Once again, it's not reality. It's only a past experience; pretty much useless to hold on to as it's not there anymore (though many wish it was), and it takes us away from living our current reality.

What keeps us from fully experiencing the present moment is all the wayward wandering and needy grasping of our minds. Generally speaking, our minds busy themselves in one of two ways:

- Milling around or ruminating over the past:
    - "I should have given him a piece of my mind when I had the chance!"
    - "If I'd followed a different path, I'd already be successful."
    - "My heart shattered into tiny pieces when she left me three years ago."
    - "I'll never experience another moment in life as good as that one."
    - "If only my Dad hadn't left when I was eight – it ruined me."

- Thinking of, planning for, or worrying about the future:
    - "I wonder if I'll lose my job."
    - "We'll get married soon, have two kids, and then I'll be happy."
    - "What will I do if I get cancer?"
    - "I bet he'll go off and have an affair with that woman from work."
    - "I'll get my Master's Degree, find a great job and then be set for the rest of my life."

The present is this moment... now... now… now. For those of us with minds conditioned to think, think, think about past and future events and possibilities, bringing attention to the present moment for more than a few seconds seems an incredibly difficult thing to do. That's because it is. Our minds race constantly with thoughts that lead us away from the present. Quieting our minds from the endless mind chatter can seem, for many, an almost impossible task. How is it possible to shift ourselves out of our compulsive past and future thinking?

A good place to start quieting this thinking monster is to get out of your head and into your body. "But I am in my body! Where else would I be?" I hear you cry. If your mind's off chasing this thought and that, you're not 'in your body', you're stuck in your head (and yes, I realise that's a part of the body – just go with me here). Bringing attention to bodily sensations helps us to become present. What does that mean? Your body is your connection to reality – it doesn't live in the past or future. It provides you with a grounding to live in presence because, unlike the mind, it provides us with a point for steady awareness. By focusing the mind on the inflow and outflow of breath, or on parts of the body (your body, not somebody else's), you start to calm the frivolous dancing of the monkey mind. One practice I find particularly beneficial when out and about is keeping attention on the sensation at the soles of my feet while walking. No need to do anything. No need to think about or analyse it. Just feel the pressure, the sensation. That's all there is to it. By keeping focused attention on a part of the body, we quieten our thoughts and calm the mind, giving ourselves a break from the incessant chatter. Simple, yet so relaxing!

Learning to live more in the present, we begin dropping the habit of anticipating what could happen and open ourselves to embracing whatever might come along. We create a mind-set that watches life move around and through us, flowing with whatever it is that comes our way. Our power comes then not in trying to control life, but in controlling our responses to what happens around us. We learn to drop expectations and detach ourselves from the need for things to be a certain way, trusting that we're more than capable of responding to whatever circumstance comes our way.

It's said that highly evolved and enlightened beings live fully in the present. Probably because they've long since realised the delusion of living anywhere but the present.

"I do not want to foresee the future. I am concerned with taking care of the present. God has given me no control over the moment following."

Mahatma Gandhi

Sure, he was lovey-dovey now, but Joanne feared someday
he might run off with that perky blonde from work.

Accepting What Is – Letting Go of What Isn't

CFs have this (almost megalomaniac) point-of-view that if the present reality isn't suitable, all they need to do is change it or escape it. By changing it, they attempt to influence or control everything to achieve outcomes that are more appropriately perfect. Or, if changing people or situations proves too difficult, they can flee by 'detaching' (read: escape, avoid, isolate, distance) from the circumstance or person altogether. In my full-on CF mind-set, I used to think that my self-professed 'detachment' was a highly evolved behaviour, drawing parallels with the higher spiritual practices of Buddha and Jesus who were able to live fully in the present. After awakening to my highly-deluded ego perceptions, I now realise this pseudo 'detachment' felt right because I was so cut off from the present and my feelings – it was my way of removing myself entirely (or at least burying myself) from the unbearable heaviness of reality (NOT unbearable lightness of being). It was my opt-out tactic, removing me further from where I really needed to be.

One of my favourite teachers is Byron Katie. In her book, 'Loving What Is', she outlines a pretty radical no BS approach to life. It's a challenging read; and if you read it more than once, you'll feel even more challenged. For CFs generally, the discomfort factor in taking in any information to do with accepting 'what is' is roughly multiplied by twenty. But what is this concept of 'loving what is'? Stemming originally from Taoist philosophy, it's essentially about stopping your struggle with reality (what is) and accepting it. It's our thoughts and beliefs that keep us stuck in a pattern of resistance to reality. In Byron Katie's words:

"The only time we suffer is when we believe a thought that argues with what is. When the mind is perfectly clear, what is is what we want."[6]

Katie gets to the core of life perspective, stating that we either accept what is in our lives or the suffering within will continue. Even awareness of the conflict that arises within us when we find it more than a bit difficult to love what is, is all grist for the mill according to Katie. The only thing we need to concern ourselves with, in her opinion, is 'our business'. What others do in their lives and what's worked out in a divine bigger picture sense, is not our business and shouldn't be of concern to us in any way, shape or form – even if it impacts us directly.

Having first come upon her book at the local library, I borrowed it, renewed it twice, and left it sitting by my bedside unread throughout that time. Then I received it as a birthday present the same year (clear message coming through here), read the first few chapters then put it down for six months. Over that time, I argued vigorously with Katie in my head, stubbornly refusing to even consider taking on board her ideas. But the concepts she presented kept milling around in the back of my mind. When I picked up the book and finished it eight months later, I was ready to hear her message.

Though still confronting, I could check out her ideas without the emotional triggers that had fired off those previous times. I'd reached a point where I still debated but didn't try to fight her concepts, even though they conflicted with societal conditioning and every defence mechanism my mind conjured up. I just couldn't argue with something so simply logical.

The flip side of 'loving what is' is letting go of what isn't – certainly one of my biggest life lessons. In order to fully accept and embrace the reality of our current life situation, we must release our rather pig-headed grasp on our preferred reality outcomes ("If she really cared, she'd work less hours and spend more time with me and the kids"; "I'm obviously more competent and qualified, I should have got that position"; "He just doesn't show he loves me like he should"). When we put lots of mind energy into complaining about how bad/unfair/not good enough things are, our efforts at changing them (if you could call it that) are completely wasted. Expecting events, people or situations to be different from how they are weighs us down and takes our energy away from where it needs to be – working out how we can respond more effectively to the situation at hand, even learning to welcome the associated possibilities.

For those of us with stubbornly rigid minds, who believe that if we hold onto a completely unrealistic idea long enough it will come to pass (i.e. probably all CFs), the thought of letting go into the void of not knowing is paramount to an explosion in the amygdala (the brain's emotional defence system). We need things to be a certain way or else it's just not good enough or out-and-out bad. There's so much of a distorted 'me' perspective going on – believing the world's trajectory has us at the very centre – we struggle hugely to understand that 'it's not all about me'. Letting go of our expectations about how things 'should' be and acknowledging that 'shit happens' at times (and that some shit, like manure, can help things grow), we can ease into a deeper appreciation of the ebbs and flows of life.

Striking a Being/Doing Balance

Plato once wrote "Know thyself" – a greater foundation for wisdom is hard to find. Before we can even consider what it looks like to get a grip on accepting reality, first we need to truly commit to setting aside some serious time to connect into who we are. When we're self-professed experts on externalities, yet spend next-to-no time or effort digging around in our own psyche, whatever knowledge we profess to have about ourselves tends to be superficial and/or limited. Even when we believe we have a sharp intellectual grasp on something, unless we've balanced that with our emotional responses to it (EQ) as well, we can never develop a wiser understanding of the subject.

Some people cop a lot of flak for being a CF when they've really got absolutely no idea how they come across to the world. Setting up space and time to practice 'beingness' helps us understand what we're made of (beliefs, values, characteristics) and how we tick (interests, priorities, motivations, triggers). Try considering it a fundamental responsibility to tune into yourself. It's close to bordering on self-neglect if we don't set aside opportunities to just be still and get to know who we are. Failing to connect in with ourselves, our general tendency is to blame others – the blinkers are on and we just can't see how we're contributing to the issue. The more self-awareness generated, the more responsibility we take on, the healthier our perspectives, the less we blame everyone else for our problems, the further we step outside the box and challenge ourselves, the more satisfaction and fulfilment we have with our lives.

Because of the CF tendency to spend a significant amount of time in our heads – lots of frantic mental activity working out strategic life plans – there's a whole lot of *doing* going on, both physically and mentally. A huge amount of time is invested by CFs in these cerebral pursuits, leaving little or no time for the much more rewarding task of self-connection. A decade ago, the notion of setting aside 'being' time was a foreign concept to me. Sure, I'd dabbled in meditation since my early twenties, but continued to grapple with a dominating monkey mind mentality. My opinion on spending quality 'being' time was along the lines of: "What a waste of time sitting around doing nothing of much use when I could be doing, planning or thinking about something more substantial." In those days, I believed the greatest contribution to my own well-being was to get more things done. Gee, how wrong was I?!

In our hyper-busy, need-to-have-more society, our lives are filled to the brim with things we need to get done. We're constantly thinking about our 'To Do' list; we're searching for time to fit everything into our tight schedules; we're juggling work, family, home duties, hobbies and downtime to make it all fit in. Somewhere along the way, my guess is after the onset of the Industrial Revolution when productivity became king, cultural and societal expectations started aligning busyness and doing with success. We wind ourselves up into a frazzle trying to get it all done and forget (or de-prioritise) the one thing that could help bring any sanity back into our life perspective – taking time to simply be. If we don't make time for stillness in our lives, using the peace and quiet to work out all our stuff, the non-stop doingness can literally take over our existence, leaving us burned out and wondering how the hell we can give ourselves a break and escape all the noise.

Obviously, in this gung ho day and age, the significant majority of our time will be spent getting things done. But there needs to be some kind of balance between time spent being and time spent doing. In dedicating certain times to capturing a few minutes (or even a whole hour) of quiet beingness, not only do we get a much needed rejuvenation boost, we're also giving our self-awareness a useful shot in the arm. Think about it... setting aside 5 or 10 minutes of peace and quiet could be the difference between crashing from major overload and sustaining a focused effort. Taking time for you – just after rising, on your lunch break, when you've stepped out to the toilet, after tucking the kids into bed, or on a weekend retreat – makes a huge impact on your overall approach to life, to say nothing of how it helps you deal with the little and 'holy crap' dilemmas that pop up along the way.

Check out some of these 'being' practices yourself:

- A few minutes focusing on the breath – practicing mindfulness;
- Tuning into a guided audio meditation;
- Sitting quietly in a place of worship or in Nature;
- Reflecting quietly on your life and what's important;
- Journaling what's happening in your life and how you feel about it;
- Bringing awareness to the sensations in your body.

Going With the Flow

When we slowly start letting go of the need for control and practice accepting what is and 'beingness', it feels a bit like taking the training wheels off a kid's bike – we don't know if we're going to stay upright, fall on our arse or crack our head open. At times, we really aren't sure whether we want to get back on the bike again if we do take a fall. But with loads of practice, a get-back-in-the-saddle attitude, and a willingness to learn how we can start trusting ourselves and others in situations that seem more than a tad risky, we eventually start feeling that sense of balance, flow and freedom integral to the letting go process.

> *"Life is a series of natural and spontaneous changes.*
> *Don't resist them – that only creates sorrow. Let reality*
> *be reality. Let things flow naturally forward in what-*
> *ever way they like."*

Lao Tzu

In learning to accept reality, we invariably come across incidents surely designed to test our progress. It could be a set of small happenings more irritable than worrying: spilling coffee on your shirt before a big interview; a burst water pipe as you're heading out the door for an appointment; misplacing your car keys; a sick kid needs minding when you've got a super-busy work day. Either that or we're presented with one of the more full-on, blood-pressure-raising varieties: a stolen wallet/passport while travelling in a remote part of the Indian subcontinent; the revelation of a partner's affair (and you're the last to find out); a traffic jam which causes us to miss an important flight; a conspiracy between work colleagues that ends up with you being fired. Whether it's a minor or catastrophically major outcome that throws our plans and expectations way off course, it's more than likely our feathers will be ruffled to a greater or lesser extent.

How I see it, going with the flow comes through bringing awareness to each moment, and accepting everything and anything that comes up; basically equating to zero resistance. When we keep our attention as much as possible on what's happening now, we become more and more comfortable with accepting what is and we eventually end up assimilating this practice into everything we do each day. Sure, there's always going to be glitches in the system. Unless we're fully self-actualised or enlightened beings there'll always be slight tugs here and there pushing us to buy into thoughts that struggle with reality. The key to stepping into the flow is diligent practice in the here and now. Training in and practicing mindfulness, building awareness at every opportunity (each day is packed full of them), literally rewires the connections within our brain, building healthy new pathways. Ever heard of neuroplasticity – the brain's ability to change? We can change the way our brain's wired through repeating healthy new thoughts and behaviours – sooner or later connections relating to the pathways supporting outdated thoughts and behaviours just drop away, leaving you with a new improved way of being.

So seemingly we're not meant to be old dogs that can't learn new tricks!

As the end of world unfolded, Tom decided now was as good a time as ever to live fully in the present.

(TWELVE)

GOING THERE FROM HERE

Choose Change or Change Chooses You

By now you should have a pretty good understanding of the CF personality as well as more than a few tips on what's needed to get out of hyper-anxious/insecurity mode and into seeing your truth and embracing the reality staring you in the face. The very idea of releasing the control strings can create a whole heap of anxiety for some. Any prospect of letting go, accepting what is, and doing whatever it takes to inject a massive shot of self-belief is more than enough to send some CFs into out-and-out overwhelm. Others may be thinking it's time to take on change – in baby steps or a mammoth leap – and start poking around murky past stuff, grappling to get a leash on the monkey mind, sorting through BS beliefs to find self-truths, all the while inching towards dropping the control reins.

Whether you choose change or stick to the status quo, the most profound impact of having read this book will be the boost to your CF understanding and self-awareness – for

Going There From Here | 167

some substantially, and others in the most unintentional and discrete of ways. The seed has been planted. Whether change crops up immediately or takes years of manure to germinate, it's sure to eventually take root and grow. Conditions have to be pretty much right for the change process to kick off, and it often takes a lot more than the simple act of reading a book for an idea to develop. Having opened yourself up to a possibility, change can start taking place regardless of whether it's welcomed with open arms or resisted outright. Changes can be so subtle as to seem imperceptible, while guiding us in the direction we need to go. In the oddest of ways, it seems at times change chooses us.

Perhaps the best motivator for diving into change is suddenly waking up to just how way overdue and urgent the need for it is. "No time for fart-arsing around", as my Dad would say. Slap yourself around more than a few times with the impacts of being a CF to wake yourself up, really understanding how debilitating these behaviours are to self and others. Then maybe you can understand just how hugely important it is to do something about it *now* – not tomorrow, or once your birthday rolls around, or post-divorce proceedings, or after things finally settle down at work – *now*! This is a 'seize the day' moment in time. The longer it takes to transition to the change process, the more time you have to talk yourself out of it (and we know how great you are at that). What follows is staying stuck in the box, a continuation of living a restrictive, isolating and self-defeating life because the impetus for change – that miniscule window of opportunity that presents itself only once in a while – disappears into a world of 'what was once considered'. Change is a scary endeavour to take on – pretty much scares the living daylights out of me and everyone else I've ever known. Mustering the guts to take on personal change shows courage – doing it often enough helps us grow from childish fiends into mature grown-ups. Otherwise we just stay stuck living out childhood behaviours in an adult body. So get the urgency of the message and do something about it today.

And if you get a little too caught up grabbing change by the horns, remember to incorporate some chill out time – balancing the being and doing elements and always bringing the focus back to the present. Keeping in mind that the intention you've set and actions you take around self-transformation will undoubtedly take you through highs and lows, and grow you as a result of them. When reflecting on change and life's uncertainties, I can't help being reminded of the 'Serenity Prayer':

> *"...give me grace to accept with serenity the things that cannot be changed, courage to change the things which should be changed, and the wisdom to distinguish the one from the other."*

> Reinhold Niebuhr

Fessing Up and Getting Accountable

One of the more challenging (yet unusually liberating) tasks you can take on is to 'fess up' about your controlling to someone who's not going to verbally pummel you into the ground if they think they can when you're baring your bits to them. Chances are, if they truly know you, their response to this revelation won't be a giant surprise (they've known it for ages), but more of a "Thank God you've finally woken up to yourself" sense of immense relief. Try not to be too disappointed by responses that don't reflect astonishment and compassion, or remarks that fail to compliment your insightful level of self-awareness. This individual has probably been on the receiving end of your behaviours many a time, and is surely grateful to finally get an opportunity to let you know just how they feel about these behaviours of yours. Prepare yourself for their venting of thoughts, opinions and feelings, which may have been pent up for years, and give yourself a big pat on the back for having the guts to open up.

Fessing up is closely associated with taking accountability. I tell someone close to me about my plans because it's one of the best ways to keep myself accountable to the things I'm committed to changing and getting done. You've put your intention out there – people remember and will keep calling you on it, unless they realise you're squarely in the no-hoper wannabe box. Keeping commitments private makes it far too easy to renege and change plans mid-stream if the going gets a bit rough or uncomfortable. What you're essentially doing is cornering yourself into a position where outside influences will keep you on the straight and narrow. The bearers of this confidential information will (hopefully) support you in not getting away with all the crappy controlling behaviours you've been addicted to in times gone by. Some people you tell will take on this new role of behavioural inspector with absolute relish, and pay back may be sought in a subtle (or not so) way.

Try not to get into too much of a fluster if some people are overly 'enthusiastic' with your efforts to transform. You may need to keep your ego in check so it doesn't lash out at what it perceives (rightly or wrongly) as an attack on your openly vulnerable state of being. People close to you will typically want to support you in being your best and fulfilling your goals and dreams, even if that means holding you to account when push comes to shove and the going gets a little difficult. Remember, if you regularly commit to something then pull out, people will think you're a bit of a loser and none of your future commitment statements will get much attention or support. So only fess up and commit to change when you've thought it through long and hard and are prepared to give yourself a no-way-out option – because that's exactly what you might get.

"Oh really? And you've only just figured this out?"

Your Support Crew

CFs typically aren't that open to asking for or receiving support from others, especially those considered skilled at getting to the core of an issue. As I've already pointed out, quite succinctly I hope, CFs have a MAJOR problem in trusting others. So when someone starts peering behind our perfectly polished veneer, the chances of maintaining a composed image are significantly reduced – with inner turmoil an almost inevitable outcome. While the possibility of a CF reaching out to someone unknown or trust-untested is extremely remote, they can ask support from those already in their circle of trust.

For CFs who muster enough courage to take the risk and score the support they need, starting off a change process is an empowering and self-affirming step. Unless we have an uncanny ability to transition ourselves through change (typically not a CF strong point), we do best by pushing ourselves out of our comfort zone and finding the assistance we need. When feeling helplessly stuck in habits and behaviours driven by a mind-set conditioned by fear, many people (non-CFs included) won't ask for help and instead stay stuck more or less where they are. Too petrified to step away from what they know, no matter how uncomfortable it is in that space, they remain victims of circumstance, having passed up their freedom to choose an alternative. So any move made to gain a little support to help step away from fear-based behaviours deserves a pat on the back as it's going against the norm to discover what's possible.

Some examples of external support sources include:

➢ A good friend is priceless when it comes to talking through issues and feelings – just make sure it's someone with healthy boundaries who has your best interest in mind.

➢ Many people balk at the thought of going into therapy, thinking it's for society's weaklings and weirdoes. But it's a fabulous way of accessing deeper self-awareness, learning different perspectives on issues and improving ways to communicate and relate to self and others. It exponentially accelerates behavioural change in an objective, supportive way.

➢ Grab a self-help book – some of the titles may sound a little odd, but the information can be gold (check out the 'Recommended Reads' list at the end of this book).

➢ Often we're so out-of-touch with our bodily feelings – a therapeutic massage (I'm thinking remedial deep tissue, not the happy-ending type) can help release tensions and pent up emotions, putting us back in touch with our bodies once more.

➢ There's a wide variety of support and self-help groups out there where members provide mutual support for each other by sharing issues and experiential knowledge – available in both a face-to-face and online capacity. No, I'm not referring to Facebook or Twitter here.

Self-support is an absolute necessity when going through any type of transition. Initially I found it quite awkward to work out how I could support myself through change. By searching online and asking a few friends what things they did, I easily gathered up more than enough tips and tools. Incorporating them into my routine was the hard part. While some people find self-nurturing activities quite natural (introverts are usually great at this), my active, do-ing nature constantly argued (still does at times) against the practicality of slotting nurturing time into my busy sched-ule. Nowadays, when I don't set aside time for being, I feel stale, uptight and frustrated – which gives me a clear signal to get back into some self-nurturing.

Here are a few starters for what could be included in a self-support model:

➢ Regular time scheduled in for meditation and reflection.

➢ Daily updates in a gratitude journal – keep it by your bed and update before sleeping.

➢ Time out to rejuvenate in Nature – almost nothing beats breathing in clean air and sucking up all those negative ions to lower stress levels and improve wellbeing.

➢ Recording your thoughts, feelings, problems, ideas in a journal allows for natural resolution of issues, new per-spectives, and a deeper self-awareness.

➢ Take a bath – preferably with gentle music, lots of bubbles and a rubber duck or two (no one has to see) – and soak up the relaxation.

➢ Life doesn't have to be push, push, push. Bring back the fun – catch a movie, play a game, throw a Frisbee, play rumble with a dog, fly a kite...

➢ Ensure your environment supports you – do whatever it takes to build a happy and healthy home, physically and emotionally.

➢ Take a break on your own – a personal retreat.

➢ Sing to your heart's content – add some funky dance moves in there too.

➢ Move that body – get outdoors and get your bod in motion – a natural feel good.

➢ Find someone to hug. If you have trouble, openly advertise free hugs.

➢ Check the fuel (food and liquid) you're putting into your body is high octane, not junk.

➢ Create something unique and special for yourself or someone you love – put you into it.

➢ Find something that makes you feel good about yourself and do it.

Activities that shake you out of habitual patterns support you in being your authentic self. When going through change, the last thing you need is to feel obligated, pressured, pushed, and resistant. Some of these actions may seem a little self-indulgent – that's because they're meant to be! So often, we busy ourselves into non-existence and forget we're meant to be enjoying this ride through life. When we dedicate time and energy to the pursuit of our own happiness, we're more likely to relax, be happy, and a lot more open to accepting change. Way better than being a serious, grumpy CF devoid of life inspiration.

Beware the Self-Saboteur!

A very important detail to remember:

When you begin a process of personal change or transition, your self-saboteur will come out to play – and not in a fun way.

While many of us are somewhat aware of our self-protector – the part that steps in and tries to keep us in check when we start veering away from the status quo – many of us are quite clueless as to whether or not we have a self-saboteur at play. The self-saboteur is a part of us that's absolutely petrified of change, doing everything in its power to scare us away from choices that go decidedly against our standard way of being. While the self-protector may try reasoning us out of a situation (e.g. "Look what I have to give up"; "Not sure this will help me in the long run"; "Don't think she's the one for me"), the self-saboteur steps in after those initial attempts have fallen on deaf ears, to drive the point home and return you to your original bearings – it's like a radical extension of the self-protector.

Self-saboteur actions connect into and reinforce those negative core beliefs which are so deep-seated you may not even be aware of them ("I'm not good enough"; "My future is hopeless"; "I'm not loveable"; etc.). By ignoring those initial self-protector warning signs, some deep-seated fears can be triggered, usually accompanied by some pretty powerful emotional reactions. These can climax into behaviours we feel compelled to follow which completely sabotage the very outcome we wanted – really shooting ourselves in the foot ("Why the hell did I say/do that?!?"). All done to fortify our core self-beliefs and avoid what it is that we most fear on an individual level. I'm now able to sense when my self-saboteur is about to stick its nose in – I tend to feel a sense of overwhelm, a bit of foggy headedness, combined with an anxiousness that sits there rumbling away waiting to explode in an irrational outburst of some sort or another. Nowadays I try to catch it before I completely lose my grip on reality.

What to do if the self-saboteur comes out to play? Try talking to it. That's right, talk to it. It's just a part of us that's particularly anxious around change and uncertainty. Don't worry; you're not going to be carted away for trying this. The most effective method of calming the anxiety is to allow that part to have a voice and be heard. The best way is to start a dialogue with your self-saboteur in a journal, writing freely about any concerns and distress that's coming up. If we were to continually believe the negativity and doomsday forecasts expressed by our self-saboteur, we would carry on living a fear-based existence and end up with a bucket of regrets at the end of our days. But if we weed out the warnings and negative spin, keep the communication avenues wide open, and put some safety supports in place, we can then take on an internal coaching role and move through whatever issues are raised.

Opening up communication with our self-saboteur offers us a fabulous opportunity to delve deeply into our most primal wounds. Keep scratching the surface of the issues raised and we may find ourselves face-to-face with our 'demons' – those shadowy memories, beliefs, thoughts and feelings we like to keep hidden away. And some issues will need a bit more support than others, so please don't ever hesitate to reach out to a professional therapist (a good one's worth their weight in gold in terms of opening up self-awareness). When we can see and accept our shadow side, we make great headway into ridding ourselves of fears and controlling. So, no matter how challenging it may be when you're self-saboteur kicks up a racket, remember that it's a great indicator that you're on the right path to self-transformation.

Having taken a few steps to address his control freakiness,
Eddie was now certain nothing further could trip him up.

Other Tips and Tools

The support tips I've covered off so far are just the tip of the iceberg in terms of tools anyone can use to move forward on their change path. In this section, I've included a few additional practices specific to CFs in working through issues around control and associated fears. The point here is to learn the art of letting go, which naturally taps into feelings of vulnerability and powerlessness for the CF. Remember to make sure you have a support model in place before you stretch yourself in these ways.

➢ In small steps, practice letting go of control. Start off with situations where you feel really quite comfortable but usually take control anyway (e.g. letting someone else choose the dinner option; handing the remote to your partner; or letting another take the kudos or limelight for a change). Always check in to see what reactions come up for you. Gradually build it up to include situations where there's some anxiety attached to the outcome (e.g. letting someone else do the driving without you giving instructions or directions; delegating a semi-important task to a work colleague to complete; or refraining from speaking out against something you disagree with). Once you've practiced letting go of control around less anxiety-rich situations, gently practice in situations where you know there will be some distress if a desired outcome isn't achieved (e.g. being open about how you feel to someone important to you; allowing someone else to take control in a situation that feels physically unsafe – like abseiling; or doing anything that stretches you out of your comfort zone).

➢ Start being really curious about life. Live in a state of wonder instead of a state of bored status quo paralysis. Ask questions, seek out answers, look at things and people in new ways, and see things from new perspectives. Stepping outside your comfort zone in this way will rapidly accelerate the growth process and start those brain neuro-pathways rewiring.

➢ Find several affirmations that support you in the direction you're heading. When I'm looking for guidance or insight on an issue, I love diving in and choosing one of Louise Hay's Power Thought Cards. Strangely enough (sceptics scorn all you wish), most of the time I choose a card perfect for my predicament.

➢ If you're involved in a conversation where someone states something you feel violently in disagreement with, STOP... PAUSE... BREATHE. Then attempt a reply that has absolutely no malicious or sarcastic intent (e.g. "That's an interesting perspective" instead of "You surely can't be serious!"). If at all possible, check in with your reaction to the situation – your thoughts, body sensations, behaviours. Ask yourself questions around what specifically set you off – try getting to the core trigger and do some enquiry on that.

- Develop empowering thoughts and habits to support yourself. Inquire into and question those beliefs, thoughts and behaviours that are unhelpful or a hindrance to your well-being – this will be of great benefit in assisting you to identify all the not-so-truthful stuff that holds you back. Be ruthless in getting to the bottom of why you think, feel and act in controlling ways.

Once a CF, Always a CF?

Having explored this subject on a very personal level for close to a decade, I've often wondered along the way whether CFs can ever achieve a state of total reformation. Addicts often refer to themselves as being addicts, even if they've been 'clean' for decades (not that I'm necessarily saying control freakiness is an addiction, mind you). Those of us who have trodden the self-awareness path have typically addressed the more obvious dysfunctional behaviours (and thoughts/beliefs behind them) which stand in the way of us leading a happy and fulfilling life. But I think for many of us, traces of those characteristics are maintained. It's almost as if our very identity (how we define ourselves) is fundamentally linked into those beliefs and behavioural patterns we've carried through the years. And dropping them altogether would lead us to the question: "Who am I now?"

The opinion I've arrived at is that it is possible to transcend (verging on the spiritual here) a CF character. I imagine (as

I haven't gone there) the self-transformation required for such a feat would be quite extreme, perhaps triggered by an event that fully wakes a person up to the impacts of their way of living and being in the world (think near-death experiences as an example). Our perceptions of the world and our place and purpose in it would also need to undergo a radical alteration. If our personalities are composed of our perceptions, beliefs, values and behaviours, and if those are extensively changed, do we lose the 'me' we've always identified with? Or do we just become transcended masters after all? Something for us all to contemplate…

"When I let go of what I am, I become what I might be."

Lao Tzu

Not the End

This may be the end of the book, but hopefully it's the beginning of a self-transformation that will blow your socks off. By committing to doing the practices in this book and inquiring deeply to build your self-awareness, there's no doubt the change train will move from its current platform on to the adventure of your life. Trust yourself. Know that you can shake the CF stigma and make meaningful and lasting change. It just takes commitment, effort and perseverance. If you have those qualities in place, the rest of what's needed will fall in line when it's meant to. And know that there will be times of fear, doubt, pain-in-the-arse frustration, anger, and sadness. If you don't go through all the crappy stuff, you'll know you need to up the ante and increase the effort you're putting in. The 'negative' stuff is all part and parcel of getting where you most want to be – living a wonderful life free from fearful inhibitions.

So, what are you waiting for? Get on with it!

APPENDIX

Questionnaire Results

#	Question	A	B	C	D
1	Generally speaking, do you believe that your way is usually the best way?	3	2	4	1
2	Your partner has a habit that really irritates you. What do you do?	4	3	1	2
3	You decide to go out with your partner/friend for dinner. You:	1	4	3	2
4	When you're in a disagreement with someone, you:	1	4	2	3
5	A work transfer requires you to move to another state or region you've never lived in before. You:	3	1	4	2
6	You make a mistake in an important hand-written form. What do you do?	2	4	3	1
7	You land an interview for a job you've always wanted. How do you prepare for it?	2	1	3	4
8	You have friends over for dinner and your partner openly states an awkward or embarrassing truth about you. You:	1	4	3	2
9	Arriving home from a two-day work conference, your partner reveals they've rearranged your favourite room. You:	3	2	1	4

10	With your kids now in their teens, you become involved in a discussion with a group of friends about the problems of kids and drugs. Afterwards, you:	1	3	2	4
11	You've decided to go on a well-deserved overseas holiday. Before you leave you:	4	3	1	2
12	Your computer crashes when you're writing an important document. You:	3	4	2	1
13	Issues within an intimate relationship force you way out of your comfort zone. You:	2	3	4	1
14	You're invited out for drinks after work with your new team members. After a couple of drinks you:	4	3	1	2
15	You receive a bill for payment that doesn't seem to be correct. You:	1	2	4	3
16	Over dinner, your partner/close friend orders a dessert you're sure they won't like, ignoring the chocolate mousse they'd absolutely love. You:	2	1	4	3
17	When your partner/friend drives the car with you in it as a passenger, you:	4	1	2	3
18	You're completely overloaded with work and are getting really stressed out. You:	1	4	3	2
19	Your partner/friend decides to do something that goes completely against your better judgement. You:	3	2	4	1
20	It's your best friend's birthday and you're struggling to find the perfect gift. You:	3	1	4	2
21	A stranger in the supermarket is about to buy a product you dislike or are vehemently opposed to (for whatever reason). You:	3	1	4	2

22	Your sister/daughter/mother/best friend reveals she's fallen in love with someone you think is completely unsuitable for her. You:	2	3	1	4
23	A shop assistant informs you they don't carry the product you're looking for in their shop. But you remember seeing it there only last week. You:	3	2	4	1
24	You often complain your partner/flatmate doesn't do their fair share of housework. When they do chip in and do something, you:	4	1	3	2
25	You're aggravated when an able-bodied driver parks in the last available disabled parking zone. You:	3	2	4	1

Recommended Reads

'Embracing Uncertainty' – Susan Jeffers

Great book! Jeffers' clear and succinct language, easy to understand concepts and supportive wisdom really do stand out in this book. I've read it several times, especially when I need a reminder to let go, and always discover something 'new' inside.

'The Power of Now' – Eckhart Tolle (also available in an audio pack)

A completely transformative book – it was for me, anyway. Simple, understandable theory and examples of what it is to be living in the present and how to be there. One of my absolute faves!

'Loving What Is' – Byron Katie

I wrote about my experience finding and coming to terms with Katie's POV in Chapter Eleven. Truly transformational! A recommended read for everyone keen to go with the flow.

'The Worry Cure: Seven Steps to Stop Worry from Stopping You' – Robert Leahy

I used to be a huge worrywart – most CFs are. This book's a real help in dealing with a worrywart nature, especially if you suffer from being unable to get to or stay asleep because of it at times. Puts things in perspective and helps you learn a lot more about yourself. Definitely some "Aha" moments in this book.

'Fear and Other Uninvited Guests' – Harriet Lerner

Lerner makes it clear that this book won't heal you of your fears, but she does offer some great examples of how people have dealt with their own fears and actions you can take to work with yours.

'The Language of Letting Go' – Melody Beattie

I usually move this daily reader book from my 'favourites' bookshelf and place it strategically on my bedside table whenever I need some extra support and words of wisdom. Waking up to it every morning during challenging life periods is a welcome inspiration and a great start to the day.

'Comfortable with Uncertainty' – Pema Chodron

This wonderful book uses Buddhist philosophy to assist you in dealing with negative thoughts and increasing awareness and self-acceptance. A comforting and supportive read.

The following three books also discuss controlling behaviours, and you may find some information to be useful…

'Controlling People' – Patricia Evans

Targeted predominantly at those people who are on the receiving end of some pretty full-on controlling behaviours, this book offers an interesting theory on why people are controlling, how to recognise when someone is controlling, and an interesting solution on what to do about it.

'The Control Freak' – Les Parrott

Parrott discusses various types of CFs, and states that anxiety is the cause of controlling behaviour. Some CFs may find this book a bit negative.

'Control Freaks' – Gerald Piaget

This book is for people who have a Control Freak in their life and want to know how to recognise, understand and deal with controlling behaviours.

Websites

The CFG website – www.controlfreaksguide.com – is regularly updated with articles, resources and musings on control freakiness.

Alternatively, there are tonnes of websites resulting from an internet search using 'control freak', 'controlling people', or 'stop being controlling' as key terms – way too many to list here, especially as the sites are endlessly changing. Do the search yourself and pick a couple of sites that take your fancy. Keep in mind the vast majority of sites lack compassion and understanding for the CF, tending to support and provide counsel for the 'victims' who feel they're being controlled. So please choose carefully to avoid traumatising yourself. I tend to prefer sites that have a psychology/psychotherapy background as I know they're generally supportive and not about to take on a demeaning approach to the subject.

ENDNOTES

1 Parrott, Les. 'The Control Freak.' Tyndale House Publishers. 2001.

2 Schnarch, Dr. David. 'Intimacy and Desire'. Scribe Publications. 2010.

3 Evans, Patricia. 'Controlling People'. 2002. Adams Media Corporation. Canada.

4 Jeffers, Susan. 'Embracing Uncertainty'. 2003. Hodder and Stoughton. London.

5 This quote is often attributed to Carl Jung.

6 Katie, Byron. 'Loving What Is'. 2002. Rider.

Lightning Source UK Ltd.
Milton Keynes UK
UKHW02f0800060918
328419UK00011B/792/P